In Straw and Story

CHRISTMAS RESOURCES FOR HOME AND CHURCH

by Joyce Miller

THE BRETHREN PRESS

Elgin, Ill.

Acknowledgements

The author and publisher are grateful to the owners of copyrighted materials who have granted permission for their use in this book, including The Church of the Brethren General Board for selections that appeared originally in Messenger, Leader, or the Focus Bulletins; The Brethren Press for selections from The Brethren Hymnal and The Brethren Songbook; the Jan-Lee Music Company for the words to "Let There Be Peace on Earth"; Tyndale House Publishers for selections from The Living Bible; and Augsburg Publishing House for a selection from Christmas Is Coming, compiled by Katherine J. Weller. Donald R. Frederick prepared the master copies of the music pages.

————

Copyright   1977, The Brethren Press

Printed in the United States of America

Library of Congress Cataloging in Publication Data
Main entry under title:

In straw and story.

    Bibliography: p.
    1. Christmas. 2. Christmas service. 3. Christmas
decorations. I. Miller, Joyce, 1932-
GT4985.I53   394.2'68282   77-4979
ISBN 0-87178-418-1

Introduction

You are invited to celebrate "in straw and story" the gift of God's son. Our varied heritage is steeped in ways of celebrating Christmas. The most meaningful experiences are those we create and live through ourselves. Because we are unique, we contribute this uniqueness to those things we do.

IN STRAW AND STORY is a potpourri of resources, music, worship services, plays, recipes, patterns for handcrafted gifts and decorations, and traditions for use in a Christ-centered celebration for individual families and for churches.

Like the straw of the manger, you will find that the gifts and decorations may be uncommon though made from the common stuff of life--things you find in your home or that which can be inexpensively purchased. With your own creative twist this "straw" can become a unique expression of love for a very special someone.

Many persons have contributed to this collection of "stories." The worship resources, plays, dramas, music, and remembrances of traditions have all been written within the past few years. Recipes are favorites from the kitchens of many friends plus my own traditional ones. Some of the resources have been published before in such periodicals as *Messenger, Leader, Agenda,* and *Association for the Arts Newsletter.* Some have never been published before. While the materials are not denominational, most contributors have come from the Church of the Brethren. We cannot thank these contributors enough for their willingness to share their creations. A list of their names will be found on the next page.

I especially wish to thank Kenneth Morse and Wilbur Brumbaugh for their editorial counsel, and Wilbur for the beautiful cover he designed. *IN STRAW AND STORY* would not have happened without their encouragement and help.

And now, read on! We hope the ideas and resources will spark your imagination, to be adapted to your own family or church situation for a joyful, Christ-centered Advent and Christmas for years to come.

Joyce Miller

To my daughters

Pat, Pam, and Paula

and with thankfulness to the following friends

Greg Bachman
Tsun Hsien Bhagat
Margaret Brown
Wilbur Brumbaugh
Nancy Curtis
Mary Cline Detrick
Steve Engle
Theresa Eshbach
Nancy Faus
Richard Gardner
Hannilori Gerdes
Ronald P. Hanft
Mildred Heckert
Helen Kauffman
Barbara Kennedy
Alan Kieffaber
Dora Klostermeyer
Jeanette Lahman
Edith Merkey
Ronald K. Morgan
Kenneth Morse
Marjorie Morse
Andrew Murray
Galene J. Myers
Lois T. Paul
Joseph Quesenberry
Dianne Rist
Lyle Roth
Esther Rupel
Helen Temple Sutherland
Margaret Thomason
West Marva District, Church of the Brethren
Ramona Whetzel
Betty White
Glee Yoder

Contents

INTRODUCTION

FAMILY AND CHURCH CELEBRATIONS FOR ADVENT

THE SONGS OF CHRISTMAS

PRAYERS, LITANIES, INVOCATIONS

PLAYS AND CANTATAS

INTERNATIONAL CELEBRATIONS AND TRADITIONS

CRAFTS OF CHRISTMAS

Advent

Family and Church Celebrations

Advent a time for family worship

The wreath of Advent comes from a desire
to express joy at the coming of Jesus "the
light of the world" into our lives. For
this reason light has to be a very important
part of the celebration of Christmas.

Advent wreaths have many variations as far as
traditions are concerned. In Germany, four red
candles are used; some countries use four white candles; some prefer four violet candles and some four
violet and white with a fifth candle in the center. The
color of violet was often used in the early church because
it signified penance. In the earliest days of Christianity, as now, Advent
was a time for penance, forgiveness, and prayer, a time to prepare the heart
for the coming of Christ.

The wreath may be placed on a table or hung from a ceiling or doorway with
ribbon.

Traditionally, the first Sunday of Advent (which is near the Feast of St.
Andrew on Nov. 29), the family gathers after the evening meal. One person
lights one of the candles. Another person chooses and reads a portion of the
scripture concerning the events of Christ's birth. Then the candle is blown
out. On the second Sunday the ceremony is repeated, but two candles are lighted, and a different scripture is read. Each week the ceremony is repeated,
adding one more candle until all are lighted, and the story is completed.

Following is a selection of Bible readings appropriate for use in Advent worship.
Programs and ideas from many different persons are presented for your use on
the pages to come.

Scriptures for the Sundays of Advent

1st Sunday: Isaiah's vision of the coming Messiah-
Isa. 2:1-5; 11:1-9; 40: 3-11.
2nd Sunday: Mary--Luke 1:26-56; Isa. 7:13-14.
Joseph--Matt. 1:18-25.
3rd Sunday: Shepherds and angels--Luke 2:8-20.
Wise men-- Matt. 2:1-12.
4th Sunday: Jesus' birth--Luke 2:1-7.
Flight into Egypt--Matt. 2:13-23.

By Glee Yoder

"Faith in Jesus as a way of life cannot
exist without rituals," states *Children's
Liturgy*, "nor, in fact, can any way of
life that has some basis in a conscious
setting of priorities. People today
can and do exist without ritual.
But man without ritual is not man
come of age; he is man without age--
no past to celebrate, no present to
explore, no future to anticipate. No
way to look at what has been, is, and
will be. No way to go beyond the
unhuman facts."

There is today a searching for authentic
ritual (or liturgy) within the Christian
family. The onus is on experiences that
do not become ends in themselves, that are
not hollow or legalistic. Authentic rituals
must carry meaning beyond themselves, the living
out of the faith convictions which the ritual
both expresses and determines.

Two liturgical expressions which may be especially
enriching in the home during Advent are a prayer wall
and a Chrismon tree. While both draw on tangible
objects to remind the family of key concerns and values,
both go beyond the thing-centeredness with which the Christmas
observance so often begins and ends.

The prayer wall may be designed simply. Poster paper, wall board, burlap, felt,
or even newsprint may be used. Decorate it according to the season if it is
of temporary material. Place the bulletin board-type prayer wall in a well-
traveled area of the home. Words naming different ways to pray -- ASKING,
THANKING, LOVING, CARING--might suggest concerns and gratitudes. Let the wall
"grow" as each member shares his ideas and as interests and concerns change.

These suggestions may give you a start. ✰ Select one psalm of the fifteen
delightfully illustrated ones from the packet "New Every Morning," distributed
by the American Bible Society.   ✰ Find snapshots of persons in the family
who are celebrating wedding anniversaries or birthdays or who face surgery or
a long illness. ✰ Includes a birth announcement, a notice in the paper of
the death of a friend, a snip of fabric from a gown made for a prom, the plane
schedule of an absent member, a sprig of pine from the Christmas tree, a symbol of achievement or promotion.

        The list could go on and on, for--
        The steadfast love of the Lord never ceases,
        his mercies never come to an end.
        Lamentations 3:22

9

The value of the prayer wall is that it can become a vital and integral part of each day, and not a onetime observance or something squeezed in.

This season offers opportunities for introducing other liturgical expressions in the family setting. Try these: Upon rising, fill the house with joyful music - popular records of "Here Comes the Sun," "Let the Sun Shine In," "Everything Is Beautiful," "What the World Needs Now Is Love," or a hymn, "Joyful, Joyful, We Adore Thee," or a carol, "Joy to the World!" ★ As the family clasps hands around the table, sing a hymn or a ballad together. ★ Read from books of the Bible: Isaiah during Advent, Luke at Christmas. If the readings are carried on into spring, turn to Jeremiah and Lamentations during Lent and to John during Holy Week. ★ Use short prayers, songs, litanies, or choral readings created by members of the family.

Liturgy belongs to families who recognize that reliving and anticipating must be done if remembering and dreaming will shape the current world. It is not that the family must be constantly coming to grips with earthshaking problems of the world or even of the family. It is looking at the everyday stuff of life that needs that added dimension of thoughtful and thankful living and recognizes the Giver of all life.

The form of your family liturgy will be most effective if it uniquely fits your family, every member of it. If existence as a family is important (and it seems we are returning to this), then it should have concrete expression. It needs to be shown and said; not talked about constantly, but celebrated; not the object of redundancy but the subject of festivity - "We are happy to be together!"

The Jesse Tree

A different kind of Advent celebration for families might be the *Jesse Tree*. This idea is adapted from a little book of Advent worship services written by Raymond and Georgene Anderson. It includes 29 Bible stories and symbols, one for each day in Advent. You may purchase this little booklet or you may create your own symbols from the suggested list of scriptures.

You might like to try a unique Advent tree for your symbols to be displayed, made from a lilac branch. The idea and procedure come from the Dale Blough family of Polo, Ill., who use the lilac branch as their Christmas tree.

On about November 25, cut a branch from a lilac bush the size and shape you wish. Put the branch in an ample container of warm water. Decorate around the container any way you wish, but make sure that the water level can be kept up at all times. Place in a warm sunny location and by Christmas day you will have a tree filled with beautiful white lilac blossoms. (It seems that even purple lilacs have white blossoms when forced in this manner.)

Make a symbol each day as part of the Advent worship you plan and have one of the family hang it on the tree at that time. Symbols may be made of layers of heavy paper, styrofoam, bakers' clay or any way you wish as long as they are not too heavy.

Not only in scripture, but in your visual experience, the prophecy of Isaiah will come true.

The Heritage Story of Jesus

Read stories about the ancestors or great-great-great-grandparents of the family into which Jesus was born. Read one each day of Advent, prepare a simple symbol, and hang it on your *Jesse Tree*. As you read the scripture, discuss what made these people great and what was their relationship to God.

1. Why are the stories of Jesus important?
   Deut. 16:4-9; Psalm 119:105; Matt. 5:6-19

2. Abraham, called by God - Gen. 12:1-3; 13:8-18

3. Abraham and Lot - Gen. 17:4-8; 22:1-19

4. Jacob's dream - Gen. 28: 10-32

5. Moses' birth - Ex. 2:10

6. Moses, called by God - Ex. 3:1-17

7. God's promise to help Moses - Ex. 4:10-17

8. The Ten Commandments - Ex. 20:1-17

9. Ruth, David's great grandmother - Ruth 1 and 2

10. The story of Ruth - Ruth 3 and 4

11. God is with David - Psalm 23

12. David and Saul - 1 Sam. 18:12-16, 28-29

13. Jonathan and David - 1 Sam. 18:1-12

14. Jonathan's son and David - 2 Sam. 9:1-13

15. Isaiah's call - Isa. 6:1-8

16. Isaiah's vision of Christ - Isa. 2: 1-5; 11:1-9; 40:3-11

17. Zachariah and Elizabeth - Luke 1:5-25

18. John the Baptist - Luke 1:57-80

19. Mary - Luke 1:26-56; Isa. 7:13-14

20. Joseph - Matt. 1:18-25

21. Jesus' birth - Luke 2:1-7

22. Shepherds and angels - Luke 2:8-20; Isa. 60:1-6

23. Wisemen - Matt. 2:1-12; Isa. 25:9

24. Simeon and Anna - Luke 2:22-40

25. Flight into Egypt - Matt. 2:13-23

(Scriptures from the West Marva District of the Church of the Brethren Christmas packet.)

Ideas: present scripture and the Christmas story in a different way!

If all the group can read, read silently and dramatize afterward, or discuss, or review audibly.

Read silently an important section and paraphrase (express it in your own words).

If it is mainly for children two and three years old, open the Bible on your lap and tell the story simply. (Make use of available pre-school Bible story books.)

The best reader reads aloud to the group.

Play synagogue school. Learn as Jesus was taught. The leader (or Rabbi) reads a phrase and the group repeats the phrase after him.

Unison reading - all read together.

Read responsively; one person and then the group, or one-half the group and then the other half.

Read verse by verse around the circle.

Read chorally: one reads the voice of one person, another reads another voice. Another or the group may read the "in between."

Pre-record scripture reading so all can listen attentively. Use these recorded devotions not only for the family, but share the recording with neighbors or persons in nursing homes.

Make and use puppets to illustrate scriptures and stories.

If everyone has a Bible, let the leader "ad lib" or make mistakes, and see if the rest of the group can catch them. You might have two sides. See which side is most alert.

Illustrate the scripture readings and/or stories and make them into a book with sentence captions beneath.

Create a Christmas banner or banners from the scriptures read.

Make up new Christmas songs or verses to old melodies, or maybe new?

Make Christmas greeting cards from scriptures to share with someone who might not get many.

(Adapted from the packet for families for Christmas by the West Marva District of the Church of the Brethren.)

13

Intergenerational Christian Education Program for Advent

by Nancy Faus

Try an intergenerational Sunday school hour for the
four weeks of Advent. Groupings should be designed to
facilitate learning experiences in which children, youth,
and adults will interact and learn together. Let all the
persons in your family feel free to sign up separately for
whatever group they may wish (3rd graders on up). The youngest
children (infants, toddlers, and 3-4 year olds) will continue in
their usual rooms. It might be best for the kindergarten, first and
second grade children to participate together as a group in the Creative
Corners grouping and then urge any interested youth and adults to join that
grouping to participate in this learning experience with them.

Each of the groups should be given the opportunity on the final Sunday of
Advent to share something with the total congregation during the church school
hour, or during the worship service where it fits well. A worship committee
may wish to write the worship service as a climax to the learning experiences.
Included may be a new carol, or interpretations of old carols, a drama, an
intergenerational musical offering, etc.

A month before Advent begins announce the classes in the church newsletter
and at least three weeks before the first meeting have attractive posters
centrally located in the church halls or parlor or narthex, describing each
class and providing sign-up sheets.

Possible classes may include:

Advent Grouping 1 - *Traditional Advent Celebrations*

Description: Come and learn about some of the traditions represented in
the congregation--how the advent season has been celebrated in the varied
national backgrounds out of which we come (German, Scandinavian, Pennsylvania Dutch, English, etc.) --with resource people helping us to focus on
each tradition studied.

Advent Grouping 2 - *Creative Corners*

Description: A variety of creative experiences in different learning
centers, as we work together on greenery crafts, simple arts and crafts,
star and toy making. Bring you own glue. Further materials will be
requested as needed.

Advent Grouping 3 - *Christmas Carols--Old and New*

A look at carols--from various countries, centuries, and customs--through
singing, listening, and playing instruments. Come, join us in making
carols of the centuries come alive in a new way.

Advent Grouping 4 - *Enacting Christmas*

Description: Opportunities for developing the Christmas story through acting, scenery, costume, etc. The Biblical drama, contemporary plays, and improvisational thoughts will be used.

Advent Grouping 5 - *Bible Study of Advent Motifs*

Description: Several Advent themes from the Old and New Testaments will be studied and set forth with a special eye to the meanings they suggest for the Advent of Christ. Biblical simulation will be used.

Advent Grouping 6 - *Alternatives*

Description: What do you celebrate at Christmas? How to you express these ideas, beliefs, feelings? Are you happy with your style of Christmas celebration? Why? Why not? This group will have an opportunity to examine conventional observances of this important Christian season and will explore ways to keep Christmas in the light of such issues as ecology, simple life, hunger, inflation, and your own concerns.

Advent Grouping 7 - *Advent Food from Hither and Yon*

Description: A chance to cook and bake Advent foods that give flavor and twang to our varied Advent traditions. Enjoy kitchen fellowship in preparation for tasting traditional goodies. Will met on a week night.

Advent Grouping 8 - *Preparing and Presenting a Musical for all ages*

Examples: THE CHRISTMAS WINDOW, by Greg Bachman

GODSEND, by Donald Marsh and Richard Avery (Fortress Press)

Advent Grouping 9 - ??? (Think up another one)

Suggestions:

Be sure to have one, two, or even three conveners for each group and have them listed with the groupings.

Be sure to have as many organizational meetings as necessary during October and November to prepare well for the classes.

Encourage participation of all ages in each class. Also urge persons to stay in the class they choose for the entire four-week period.

Advent Family Cluster Groups

For an intergenerational, enlarged family celebration during Advent, try family cluster groups in your church. Ask families who would like to gather with others on Sundays during Advent to sign up on a posted sheet. Then have a committee (which has given this idea good publicity and takes care of the organization and supplies) form groupings that take into consideration children, youth, young married, middle aged, and retired people. Keep groups to around twelve to fourteen persons.

Arrange for each family cluster group to meet in the home of one of its participants (the group may choose to change the host home each week) for a two-hour period, preferable over the supper or noon hour. Within that time, plan to share in three mutual experiences together, in whatever order the group prefers:

a) eating a simple meal together--may include soup, cracker, tea-coffee-
   water, jello or fruit (Divide contributions of food between the
   participants).

b) working on a meaningful Advent project together--
   making a banner for the church sanctuary
   writing a litany for the church service (maybe even for the Christmas
     eve service)
   composing a Christmas carol
   making a creche
   creating a worship center, etc.

   The most important points are that all ages in the cluster group
   should feel and be a part of the project and that the results be
   shared with the entire church.

c) experience a worship time together. An example of such used at York
   Center Church of the Brethren (ILL.) in 1974 follows.

First Sunday - The Candle of Hope

Scripture   Luke 1:26-33

Carol   *To Us a Child of Hope Is Born*

Family discussion on the meaning and importance of hope.

Sentence prayers of hope by the entire family.

Lighting the Candle of Hope   (by a child)

All: *Together we light the Candle of Hope*

One: May God, the source of hope, give us all hope for a better world, and
   hope to those in our world who are hungry, homeless, and in anguish and
   despair.

Carol   *O Little Town of Bethlehem*

Unison prayer (St. Francis of Assisi)

Lord, make us instruments of thy peace.
Where there is hatred, let us sow love.
Where there is injury, pardon.
Where there is discord, union;
Where there is doubt, faith;
Where there is despair, hope;
Where there is darkness, light.
Where there is sadness, joy.
        We pray this in the name of Jesus Christ. Amen.

Second Sunday - The Candle of Peace

Lighting of the first Advent candle

Scripture   Luke 2:8-14

Carol   *Silent Night, Holy Night*

Family discussion on the meaning and importance of Peace.

Sentence prayers of Peace by the entire family.

Lighting the Candle of Peace   (by a child).

All: *Together we light the Candle of Peace.*

One: May God, the source of peace, give us all peace - in our families, our
   church, our communities; between nations, races, and generations.

Song *Let There Be Peace on Earth,* by Sy Miller and Jill Jackson

Let there be peace on earth   *Let peace begin with me.*
And let it begin with me;   *Let this be the moment now.*
Let there be peace on earth,   *With ev'ry step I take,*
The peace that was meant to be.   *Let this be my solemn vow:*

With God as our Father,   *To take each moment and live each moment*
Brothers all are we.   *In peace eternally.*
Let me walk with my brother   *Let there be peace on earth*
In perfect harmony.   *And let it begin with me.*

(Copyright 1955 by Jan-Lee Music. Used by permission. The word "neighbor"
may be substituted for "brother.")

Unison Prayer (St. Francis of Assisi) (see first Sunday)

Third Sunday - The Candle of Love

Lighting of the first and second Advent candles

Scripture   Luke 2:6-7, John 3:16

Carol *Away in a Manger*

Family discussion on the meaning and importance of love

Sentence prayers of love by the entire family

Lighting the Candle of Love (by a parent)

All: *Together we light the candle of love.*

One: May God, the source of love, hear our prayers of love, and help us not only to *feel* loved but to *share* that love with our brothers and sisters throughout the world, wherever and whoever they may be.

Carol *Long Ago There Was Born*

Unison prayer (St. Francis of Assisi) (see first Sunday)

Fourth Sunday - The Candle of Joy

Lighting of the first, second and third Advent candles

Scripture   Luke 2:8-17

Carol *Joy to the World*

Family discussion on the meaning and importance of joy

Sentence prayers of joy by the entire family

Lighting the Candle of Joy (by grandparent or parent)

All: *Together we light the Candle of Joy.*

One: May God, the source of joy, give joy to our hearts and our lives so that we may share that joy with others.

Carol *Hark! the Herald Angels Sing*

Unison prayer (St. Francis of Assisi) (see first Sunday)

Christmas Eve - The Candle of Christ

Lighting of the four Advent candles

Scripture   Luke 2:1-20

Carol *O Come, All Ye Faithful*

Family discussion on the birth of Christ and his importance in history and in our lives

Sentence prayers of thanksgiving

Unison prayer: *Thank you, God, for the four Advent candles and the Candle of Christ. And thank you, for the weeks of sharing that many families have had around their light and warmth. Help us to keep our lights shining so that the world may find more Hope, Peace, Love and Joy. Through Jesus Christ, the light of the world. Amen.*

Lighting the Candle of Christ

All: *Together we light the candle of Christ.*

One: May God the Father and Jesus Christ his son live within us and work through us, now and always.

Carol   *O Little Town of Bethlehem*

Closing prayer (unison, St. Francis of Assisi. See first Sunday.)

    Be sure to have an Advent wreath that can be lighted each week
    available to each family cluster group. Three purple ones and
    one pink candle are used in many liturgical worship settings, or use
    four purple candles (white is for Christmas eve or Christmas day -
    most appropriately lit in the Christmas eve service). The Advent
    committee should take responsibility for providing the candles from
    their working budget.

Throughout these weeks be sensitive to including children on an equal basis
in the worship time, project, and meal time, giving all the opportunity for
input.

The Christmas eve church service should then be a family worship service,
incorporating "gifts" that have been made in the family cluster groups,
with the Advent committee and pastor creating the elements of the service
out of the experiences of the groups. As a part of the church service use
the last of the Advent family worship periods together as a congregation.

SUGGESTIONS: If your church traditionally has a Hanging of the Greens on the
first Sunday of Advent, continue to do so, ending with a worship experience
for the entire congregation. An individual family may be used to lead the
corporate body in the first worship experience - The Candle of Hope.

Give out the Advent family worship bulletins to everyone in your congregation.
If there are families who cannot participate in a cluster group on a weekly
basis, encourage them to join in when they can; if they cannot make that
commitment for any Sunday, encourage them to take time out at home each
Sunday to celebrate the coming of Christ in their own family worship time.

do your own thing

Christmas will be a very meaningful experience within the life of the church when members have the opportunity to participate in
the total experience.

Following is a suggested idea that has
been experienced in a small local congregation. It was not only a good experience for Christmas eve, but also a
learning tool to teach about the times,
the culture, and persons involved in
the birth of Christ.

The experience is called CHRISTMAS--BC 1.
It begins the last Sunday of November, using
the learning center approach in a four-week
unit of the church school. Interested persons of all ages divide into spec-
ific interest areas of study and work to develop the celebration that emerges
on Christmas eve. The divisions used are *music, drama, costuming and props.* The Biblical stories surrounding the birth, along
with other resources telling about customs, people, foods, and music of the
land, are used as resources for the study in preparation for individual interpretations of the Nativity.

    The thrust of the three groups is as follows: *The music group*
    as do all the groups, begins with scripture, investigates types of mu-
    sic and musical instruments of that time, and studies different music-
    al interpretations used since then in telling the Christmas story. A
    very meaningful part of this study is the experience of writing a
    Christmas carol. The carol "Clip-Clop" included was written in the
    study.

The Drama group prepares the literary materials to be used and very
early in the study needs to develop a skeleton story line so that the last
two weeks the prop and costume people can put their knowledge to work. The
story line would then be further developed, perfected, and put into drama
form. Needless to say, there must be close communication between guide persons in each of the three groups so that it can all hang together, even though
it is not of primary concern that this become a professional production on
Christmas eve. In the study presented, slides were taken of the progress of
each group and then made part of the final celebration.

Costuming and prop people have the unique opportunity to study the
cultural life of the people of Jesus' time, their foods, homes, clothing, eco-
nomics, travel, religious and political observances. It is fun to develop a
Palestinian meal, make pottery lamps, etc. This group could contribute a snack
of Bible foods for planning get-togethers or final rehearsal along with preparing for the needs of the celebration on Christmas eve. Props need not be ex-
tensive. Simple touches to street clothes may be used, of if you wish, authentic costume--no bathrobes, please!

This type of program is best suited to pantomime, using readers, voice choirs and music as the cohesive and verbal contributions. This way an undue amount of time need not be spent on learning lines, and the bulk of time can be spent on actually learning about the Christmas adventure.

Following is the script of the Christmas celebration that evolved from the experience of the Franklin Grove Church of the Brethren. It is not so unusual in content, but the beautiful part is that everyone had an opportunity to share in the history and background of a very meaningful birthday party on Christmas eve.

☆ ☆ ☆

Christmas BC-1

PRELUDE

HYMN: "O Come, All Ye Faithful," sung by congregation and interpreted in dance.

CHORAL READING: (with light and heavy voice of the choir alternating. Lights dimmed) . . ." The time is coming, says the Lord, when I will place a righteous branch upon King David's throne."

He shall be a king who shall rule with wisdom and justice and cause righteousness to prevail everywhere throughout the earth. And this is his name: The Lord of righteousness. (Jeremiah 23:5-6)

For unto us a child is born; unto us a Son is given; and the government shall be upon his shoulder. These will be his royal titles: Wonderful, Counselor, the Mighty God, the everlasting Father, the Prince of Peace.

His ever-expanding, peaceful goverment will never end. He will rule with perfect fairness and justice from the throne of his father David.

He will bring true justice and peace to all the nations of the world. This is going to happen because the Lord of Heaven has dedicated himself to do it! (Isaiah 9:6-7)

READER:
And in the year 1976 we have prepared for the coming of the Lord Jesus Christ in many ways. We now share on film our preparation for this day. (Lights off and slides showing groups in work and study, preparing and learning about Christ's birthday with narration which needs to be very simple.)

HYMN: "Silent Night" sung by congregation (during this carol, actors may leave quickly to prepare for drama. They may be already costumed and seated in the congregation ready to come forward quietly at the appropriate time.)

MUSICAL INTERLUDE: Use carols or instrumental pieces of middle Eastern origin to set tone for drama to follow.

---

*Scripture reading taken from The Living Bible, copyright 1971 by Tyndale House Publishers, Wheaton, Ill. Used by permission.

READER 1:

That night some shepherds were in the fields outside the village, guarding their flocks of sheep (Shepherds appear while music of "While Shepherds Watched Their Flocks" is played).

Suddenly an angel appeared among them, and the landscape shone bright with the glory of the Lord. They were badly frightened, but the angel reassured them (acted in pantomime).

READER 2:

Don't be afraid! I bring you the most joyful news ever announced and it is for everyone! The Savior-yes, the Messiah, the Lord--has been born tonight in Bethlehem!

READER 1:

How will you recognize him? You will find a baby wrapped in a blanket lying in a manger!

READER 3:

Suddenly, the angel was joined by a vast host of others--praising God: "Glory to God in the highest heaven, and on earth peace for all those pleasing him." (Angels appear to join with shepherds to form a choir that will interpret the next section of the drama in music).

READER 1:

When this great group of angels had returned to heaven, the shepherds said to each other, "Come on! Let's go to Bethlehem! Let's see this wonderful thing that has happened, which the Lord has told us about.

*CAROL: "Clip-Clop" (written and sung by the angel-shepherd choir)

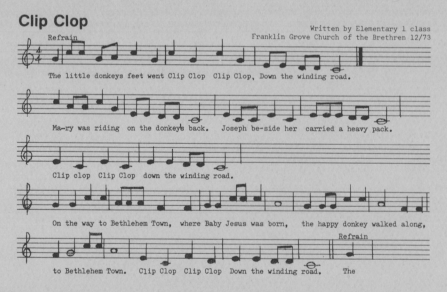

Clip Clop

Written by Elementary 1 class
Franklin Grove Church of the Brethren 12/73

Refrain

The little donkeys feet went Clip Clop Clip Clop, Down the winding road.

Ma-ry was riding on the donkey's back. Joseph be-side her carried a heavy pack.

Clip clop Clip Clop down the winding road.

On the way to Bethlehem Town, where Baby Jesus was born, the happy donkey walked along,

Refrain

to Bethlehem Town. Clip Clop Clip Clop Down the winding road. The

READER 3:

They ran to the village and found their way to Mary and Joseph. And there was the baby, lying in the manger. (Spot transfers to a different level of the stage where a crude manger filled with straw is placed. Mary and Joseph appear and place the baby in the manger)

22

CAROL: "Mary Had a Baby"   (by angel-shepherd choir)

HYMN: "Away in a Manger"   (by congregation)

CAROL: "Friendly Beasts"   (by angel-shepherd choir)

(As readers continue, the shepherds quietly leave, going into different parts of the sanctuary and being seated.)

READER 2:
The shepherds told everyone what had happened and what the angel had said to them about this child. All who heard the shepherds' story expressed astonishment, but Mary quietly treasured these things in her heart and often thought about them.

READER 1:
Then the shepherds went back again to their fields and flocks, praising God for the visit of the angels, and because they had seen the child, just as the angel had told them.

READER 2:
Now when Jesus was born in Bethlehem of Judea in the days of Herod the King, behold, wise men from the East came to Jerusalem, saying "Where is he who has been born king of the Jews? For we have seen his star in the East, and have come to worship Him."

READER 3:
When Herod the King heard this, he was troubled, and all Jerusalem with him: And assembling all the chief priests and scribes of the people, he inquired of them where the Christ was to be born.

READER 4:
"In Bethlehem of Judea: For so it is written by the prophet: And you, O Bethlehem, in the land of Judah, are by no means least among the rulers of Judah: For from you shall come a ruler who will govern my people Israel. Then Herod summoned the Wise Men secretly and found out from them what time the star appeared: And he sent them to Bethlehem, saying "Go search diligently for the child, and when you have found him bring me word, that I too may come and worship him."

READER 2:
When they had heard the king they went their way; and lo, the star which they had seen in the east went before them, till it came to rest over the place where the child was.

HYMN: "We Three Kings,"   sung by congregation.   (Wise men enter and slowly proceed down center aisle to approach the creche)

READER 1:
When they saw the star, they rejoiced exceedingly with great joy: and going into the house they saw the child with Mary his mother, and they fell down and worshipped him.

Then, opening their treasures, they offered him gifts, gold and frankincense and myrrh. And being warned in a dream not to return to Herod, they departed to their own country by another way.

HYMN: "Joy to the World," sung by congregation. (during the singing the Wise Men leave the creche and return to different places in the congregation.)

At this time all actors rise and begin to sing the chorus of "Go Tell it on the Mountain," leaving their seats and encouraging the congregation to join in and follow them out of the sanctuary and into the Christmas night.

Other resources: "The Good News," published by the American Bible Society; "Cookbook of Goods From Bible Days", by Jean & Frank McKibbin, Voice Publishers, Northridge, California; "Life in Bible Times," National Geographic Society

The Chrismons Tree

A family night celebration preparing
the church for Christmas

As families arrive, they may be divided into family
groups or other divisions of four to six people. Materials
including white felt or heavy white double knit, gold trims,
sequins, buttons, etc. should be available on work tables with
scissors, glue, needles, and thread and pieces of paper to create
or duplicate the symbol patterns. At least one pattern and its interpretation should be given to each group. Symbols may also be made of styrofoam, but it is more expensive, and you would need a foam cutter which
could be purchased from a craft or hobby store. This medium is not practical for large groups but would be a possibility for a family Chrismons
tree.

The patterns enclosed (1 sq. = 2") may be used or you may wish to create your
own designs from the interpretation sheet. Ornaments may be made by cutting two pieces of material using the pattern. They then may be sewn or
glued around the edges, leaving a small opening to stuff them slightly to
give a three-dimensional appearance. Old nylons that have been cut into
pieces of cotton or polyester batting may be used. After stuffing, finish
fastening edges and decorate with the gold trims, etc. Use your imagination! Make hooks with loops of gold trim or use little wire hooks made for
Christmas ornaments.

Duplicates of a symbol may be prepared by each group to make a well decorated
tree. These can be added after the celebrative service below, or if you
wish, write one of your own. It is helpful to have prepared ahead of time
a sheet or bulletin insert with the names and interpretations of symbols.

While most groups are making symbol ornaments, several persons will need
to prepare a tree in a firm holder and decorate it with tinsel ropes of gold.

When the Chrismons are finished, have the groups gather around or near the
tree with their creations and an appointed member of each group to share
its meaning at the appropriate time.

Celebration of the Chrismons

(As families are seated around or near the prepared tree, sing one or more
of the following suggested Christmas hymns. The two "CELEBRATORS" voices
should be in contrast if possible, one light and one heavy, to give an added dimension to the reading.

"Long Ago, There Was Born" 127 in The Brethren Hymnal, stanzas 1, 2;
"To Us a Child of Hope is Born" 123 in The Brethren Hymnal, stanzas 1, 2;
"Brightest and Best of the Sons of the Morning" 144 -- all stanzas.

25

CELEBRATOR I: As we gather to begin the celebration of the birth of our Lord
    Jesus Christ, we join thousands of churches all over the world,participa-
    ting in the custom of the Chrismons Tree. Christians from Saudi Arabia,Viet-
    nam, Sweden, India, Newfoundland, Argentina, Japan, and Ethiopia, as well
    as every state in the U.S. and all the continents of the world except Ant-
    arctica have made Chrismons ornaments to celebrate the nativity of our Lord.

CELEBRATOR II: The term Chrismons is a compound of Christ and monogram. Sym-
    bols of their faith were used by early believers in days when it was danger-
    ous to be a Christian.

CELEBRATOR I: Followers of Jesus resorted to secret signs to keep from reveal-
    ing themselves unnecessarily to the foes of Christianity. At such times
    Christians would have to worship in secret, and visiting Christians would
    find their way in large underground passageways to the worship center by
    simply looking for the fish symbol on the wall, pointing the direction in
    which they were to go.

CELEBRATOR II: Chrismons is just that -- a sign or monogram of Christ.

CELEBRATOR I: Chrismons Tree decorations are made in white or combination of
    white and gold. White is the liturgical color for Christmas because it
    symbolizes our Lord's purity and perfection. Gold refers to his majesty
    and glory. (For use in the home, tiny lights may be added to the tree.
    They are symbols of Christ, the light of the world.)

CELEBRATOR II: Let us now decorate with the symbols we have created and share
    the meanings they represent about our Lord.

CELEBRATOR I: (Name the symbols one at a time giving time to have each hung
    on the tree and for the explanation by chosen members of each group. When
    all are completed, continue with the following benediction.)

CELEBRATOR II: Heavenly Father, as we are made more aware of the sign lan-
    guage of our faith, may our spiritual lives be deepened. Hopefully, the
    beauty and meaning of the Chrismons Tree will remind us at this busy
    Christmas season of your majesty and your perfect gift to us all.

CELEBRATORS I & II: Amen

ALL: Amen

ALL SING: "Joy to the World," stanzas 1, 2 & 5

(A social hour might follow with symbol shaped sugar cookies and hot choco-
    late or fruit punch.)

The idea of the Chrismons tree was the inspiration of Mrs. Harry W. Spencer
    of the Lutheran Church of the Ascension, Danville, Virginia.

VARIATIONS: Chrismons ornaments may be made by church school classes as part
    of their study of Christmas and used as part of a special Advent program,
    such as Hanging of the Greens. Or they may be adapted for use in family
    advent worship, preparing one symbol each day or week for a Chrismons tree
    at home.

Identification and explanation of symbols

for use at Christmas

1. <u>Chalice</u>. Latin for "cup" used to administer communion. The cup is also a symbol of service.

2. <u>Bread</u>. Symbol of the body of Christ used in the communion.

3. <u>Tub & Towel</u>. Symbols of the service portion of the Love Feast observed as a sacramental service by church members in their desire to live and observe the tenets of the New Testament as closely as possible. (Acts 19:4; John 13:2-11)

4. <u>Fish</u>. From the Greek letters IXOYC, meaning Jesus Christ, God's Son, Savior.

5. <u>Alpha</u> and <u>Omega</u>. First and last letters of the Greek alphabet. Used together they symbolize the everlasting nature of Christ's divinity. (1 Rev. 1:11)

6. <u>Crown</u>. "King of Kings". (Matt. 2:2)

7. <u>Anchor</u>. Anchor of the sour. (Heb. 6:19)

8. <u>Chi Rho</u>. A Christogram, the abbreviation of XPICTOC, Christos. A familiar symbol used on paraments in Europe during the Middle Ages and seen today on altar cloths and vestments in churches.

9. <u>Two turtle doves</u>. Jesus' experience in the temple. (John 2:14-22)

10. <u>Candle</u>. Jesus is the light of the world. (Matt. 5:14)

11. <u>Epiphany star</u>. 5-pointed star. Both terms, the "day star" and "morning star," have reference to Christ. (1 Peter 1:19)

12. <u>Celtic Cross</u>. Used in northern Europe as a symbol of Christ's passion. The circle behind the cross arms denotes the everlasting divinity of our Lord.

13. <u>Star of David</u>. Symbol of God the Father. Jesus was born of the house of David.

14. <u>Triuna</u>. Symbol of the Trinity – the three-fold nature of God.

15. <u>Ship</u>. Symbol of our heavenward voyage, the voyages of the disciples, and the journey of our Brethren ancestors out of oppression into the new world. Symbol of the church in its travels from Germany to the new world, its missionary journeys to Denmark, India, China, Africa, Ecuador, and other places; symbolic also of the cattleboats that delivered cattle to other countries of the world after World War II (Heifer project).

1.   2.   3.   4.

5.   6.   7.   8.

9.   10.   11.   12.

13.   14.   15.   16.

17.   18.   19.   20.

21.

22.

23

24.

25.

26.

27.

28.

29.

30.

31.

32.

33.

16. **Egg.** Resurrection, because it contains new life.

17. **Descending dove.** The Holy Spirit.   (Matt. 3:16)

18. **Latin Cross.** Lower portion twice as long as the upper.

19. **Maltese Cross.** Arms broadened to made two points each. Emblem of John the Baptist. The eight points symbolize the beatitudes. (Matt. 5:3-10)

20. **Twelve pointed star.** Symbol of the twelve tribes and the twelve apostles.

21. **Parish Volunteer Service.** A new way for persons to devote their lives to service within the local church.

22. **Plain wide brim hat and prayer bonnet.** Worn by Brethren as outward symbols of their belief in a simple and plain ways of life.

23. **Triangle with water.** Trine immersion was adopted by Brethren as the approved method of baptism from their search of the Scriptures. The first baptism in America was held in 1723 in the Wissahickon Creek by Peter Becker, the first Brethren minister in America.

24. **The illuminated letter** S. Similar to ones printed by Christopher Sauer, Sr., who though never a member of the Church of the Brethren, was sympathetic to its point of view. He printed the first German language newspaper and Bible in America on his press.

25. **BVS.** A service-oriented program created to give opportunity for service to the world. Persons may devote one or two years or more of their lives in full Christian service through many programs.

26. **Dove.** The emphasis on a life of peace by Brethren has been especially important. Many persons throughout the history of the church have refused military service and refused to take human life. Many like John Naas and Ted Studebaker have died for their stands for peace and concern for mankind. CPS (civilian public service) and other service programs were sponsored by Brethren and approved by the U.S. Government as alternatives to military involvement.

27. **Cup-plate-towel.** Symbols of the Love Feast celebrated first by Brethren in the United States on Christmas Day in 1723. The Love Feast is an ordinance fashioned after Jesus' Last Supper with his disciples before his crucifixion. It includes three segments; the service of feet washing, the meal, and the bread and cup communion.

28. **A doctor's bag and Bible.** The tools of John Kline's trade as he rode 30,000 miles of his famous horse Nell to serve as moderator, preacher, and doctor on both sides of the Civil War.

29. Hope-Joy. Symbol of the joy and hope expressed in worship of our Lord. Used as a worship symbol for the 1968 Annual Conference of the Church of the Brethren. The symbol was created by Wilbur Brumbaugh and is an adaptation of an early Egyptian symbol for hope. Annual conferences have decided policy and provided spiritual inspiration for the Brethren since the early years of the denomination. The yearly "Big Meeting" has struggled with interpreting the Word and has offered a meeting ground for the family at large.

30. Laying on of hands. A service on commitment and dedication for those entering Christian service and a blessing for those needing God's special strength.

31. The shaped note. Symbolic of the Brethren love of music. Many hymns were "lined" as a way of singing without a hymnal. (The words are sung a line at a time by the chorister ahead of the congregation.) Conrad Beissel, once a Brethren leader, later formed a monastic community known as the Ephrata Cloisters and composed seven and eight-part music. One of the first Brethren hymnals using shaped notes was edited by H. R. Holsinger and published in 1892.

32. Lamp. Symbol of Jesus Christ, the light of the world.

33. The octagon. The eight founders of the Church of the Brethren, of whom Alexander Mack was named the first minister and early organizer.

Each grid square in the diagram equals 2" square. Symbols should be made from heavy white material such as felt and decorated with scraps of gold trims. White is the symbolic color of Christmas and purity. Gold denotes the divinity of Christ the King. A variation in color might be considered when creating the heritage symbols. They might be made of plain fabrics of earthy colors or carved in soft wood.

For other Christian symbols that might appropriately celebrate Christ's birth, consult the paper "Christian Symbols," by Miller, or create your own symbols from the Scriptures that speak to you about the life of Christ.

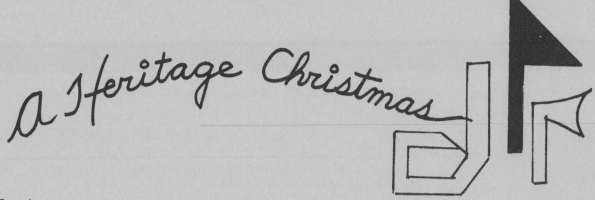

A Heritage Christmas

In the year of the Bicentennial much thought and consideration went into a study of the history of our nation. It made us aware not only of our nation's history, but brought many of us into a search for our own history as members of the Church of the Brethren. In the United States, Christmas has a special significance for Brethren, since on Christmas day in 1723, the first baptism by trine immersion was held in the Wissahickon Creek. The six persons who had requested baptism walked through the woods to break the ice and become the first baptized members of the Church in America. After the baptism they gathered for a love feast celebration.

Many dramas have been written in recent years about our heritage. One which was written to celebrate the Nampa, Idaho, congregation's 75th Anniversary has been adapted for your use.

Another possibility for heritage celebration would be to adapt the idea of the Chrismons into a Brethren Heritage Tree. Symbol ornaments could be made at a family night or in special church school classes studying heritage. These -- used to decorate a tree during a special decorating party or worship service -- could be very meaningful and informative.

Suggestions for symbols best suited for use on the heritage tree and their interpretive paragraphs are numbers 3, 15, and 21 through 33 in the section of this book on IDENTIFICATION AND EXPLANATION OF SYMBOLS FOR USE AT CHRISTMAS. A very old *parting* hymn found in the 1882 edition of *A Collection of Hymns and Sacred Songs of the Brethren of the Old German Baptist Church*, and a benedictory scripture are included as resources. Using your creativity, these components may be gathered together as a celebration of our heritage for Christmas.

You are encouraged to create symbols of your own relating to meaningful events in your church history to replace or add to the ones suggested here. Since Brethren have had a history of being concerned about simple forms of living and dress, take this into consideration when making symbols. Plain earthy colors, shades of browns, golds, blues, black and white would be best to use. Symbols may be made of plain fabrics sewn and slightly stuffed with old nylons or cotton batting, or carved of balsa wood or soft pine if you have whittlers available. Corn husks and straw are also appropriate media to use. Another approach would be to make them of baker's clay or a very stiff cookie dough. (If you want to eat the cookies later, seal each in a little plastic pack for hanging on the tree. An after Christmas party will take care of decorations with nothing gone to waste!) Recipes and how to's are in the craft section of this book.

It is appropriate that all symbols referring to Christ would be in white or white and gold as these are representative of his purity, perfection, majesty, and glory.

Lord, At This Closing Hour
6686

Unknown   tune by Joyce Miller

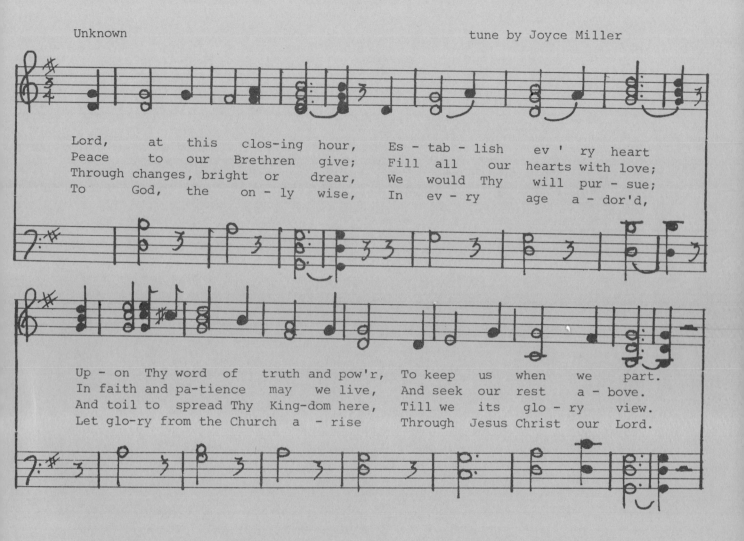

Lord,   at   this   clos-ing hour,   Es - tab - lish   ev ' ry heart
Peace   to   our   Brethren give;   Fill all   our   hearts with love;
Through changes, bright or drear,   We   would Thy   will pur - sue;
To   God, the on - ly wise,   In   ev - ry   age   a - dor'd,

Up - on Thy word of   truth and pow'r, To keep us   when   we   part.
In faith and pa-tience   may   we live, And seek our rest   a - bove.
And toil to spread Thy King-dom here, Till we   its   glo - ry view.
Let glo-ry from the Church a - rise   Through Jesus Christ our Lord.

Scripture: "In the midst of the church will I sing praise unto Thee".
Heb. 2:12

Additional resources available: Heritage Learning Curriculum published by the
Church of the Brethren 1975 - Editor - Wilbur E. Brumbaugh - Brethren Press
1451 Dundee, Elgin, Illinois 60120

A Christmas to remember

adapted from a play written by Ramona
Whetzel for the 75th Anniversary of the Nampa,
Idaho, Church of the Brethren.

(There should be a two-level stage, if possible. One has students and minister seated around a table. A teacher stands at the end of the table, sitting after the first few lines. The lower level should be in view of students and audience for the pantomime sections of the drama.)

TEACHER: Many things concerning history have been happening as we have seen on television and heard about in school concerning the Bi-centennial celebration of our country. It has caused us to do some thinking about the history of our own church. I've asked our minister to join us to help answer some of our questions.

BECKY: I know our country is 200 years old, but what does that have to do with our church and Christmas?

MINISTER: Not too many years ago--in fact in 1973, our denomination had an anniversary. On Christmas day of that year the Church of the Brethren was 250 years old in America!

DONNIE: 250! WOW! That's older than my mom!

LYNETTE: But I thought the Church of the Brethren started in Germany.

MINISTER: Right, Lynette. It did. It began in Schwarzenau, Germany, in the late summer of 1708, when Alexander Mack, Sr. and seven other persons were baptized in the Eder River. Like many other religious groups of that time, the Brethren were often persecuted because of their beliefs, but the church grew in Germany over the next ten years. Finally, in 1719, a small group of families under the leadership of Peter Becker sailed for America. They settled at Germantown, near Philadelphia. Can you guess why they chose Pennsylvania?

BECKY: Because the Quakers in the Pennsylvania Colony were tolerant of other religious groups. We studied that in history.

MINISTER: Yes, many groups found shelter in Pennsylvania. For the first several years after the Becker party settled in Germantown they were busy making a new life for themselves. They had to have homes and a way to make a living. Some of them were tradesmen and had the task of setting up for business in a new country.

34

TEACHER: And can you imagine how hard that might be when not everybody in the community spoke your language!

MINISTER: Yes, living in the new world certainly presented some challenges to those early settlers and I'm sure they were sometimes discouraged and lonely. They had left behind close friends and relatives whom they must have missed very much, especially at times like Christmas. And they probably missed the church fellowship they had left in Germany, too. I can imagine that as Christmas came each year they often remembered the church bells pealing in their home villages on Christmas Eve and the hymns they used to sing.

(Sister sits trimming candles. As music begins she pauses and looks into space. As music fades she wipes her eyes and returns to her work, German music.)

TEACHER: Can you imagine what it would have been like to spend Christmas in the Pennsylvania colony? We don't know exactly what Christmas customs the Brethren settlers brought with them, but we know that many of our traditions like the tree and the advent wreath come to us from Germany. No doubt your mother would have taught you some songs about the Christ Child and you would have surely had some special candles to light for Christmas.

(Children enter carrying greens. Mother helps them arrange advent wreath with candles she has been trimming. Quiet German music.)

LORI: Why didn't the Brethren start a church right away? Then they could have gone to church on Christmas eve.

MINISTER: We don't know exactly why it took them four years to get around to organizing. It may have just been all the adjustments to their new life. We do know that some simple meetings were being held in homes by 1722, and that by 1723, six persons had requested baptism. Now they clearly needed some kind of organization and a leader. They must have prayed about it a great deal. Perhaps they even wrote to Alexander Mack, still living in Europe, for advice. We know that letters were exchanged between the two groups; and whether or not they contained direct suggestions, they undoubtedly held words of encouragement.

(Youth group sits listening as Becker stands with letter in hand.)

At last a meeting was held and the decision was made to organize a congregation. Peter Becker was chosen elder. Seventeen persons who had been baptized before coming to America would form the nucleus of the new congregation, to be joined by the six persons who had requested baptism.

(Men of group gesture toward Becker. Group leaves.)

TEACHER: And it didn't matter to them that it was winter and they had no indoor pool for baptism. They would be baptized in the river, even if they had to break the ice!

MINISTER: That's right. On Christmas Day, 1723, they walked through the woods to Wissahickon Creek for their service, the first recorded baptism

by trine immersion in America. I'd like to read you a description of that
service by M.G. Brumbaugh, one of our major Brethren historians. This is
from a book called The Brethren In Colonial America.

*(Minister reads p. 62, paragraph 3. As he reads, the youth group gathers
around Peter Becker and kneeling brother.)*

DONNIE: Boy, it must have been cold in that water!

MINISTER: I'm sure it was, but those early Brethren believed they were doing
   God's will. So far as we know, none of them died from the experience.

BECKY: What did they do then?

MINISTER: They went to the house of one of the members, John Gomorry, and
   after they had changed into dry clothing and gotten warm they held a love
   feast and communion service.

LYNETTE: I'd like to have been there that day.

TEACHER: Yes, I can imagine all the children watched and listened to all the
   things that happened that day and remembered them for a long time.

LOREN: What was their love feast like?

MINISTER: Would you like to hear what Brumbaugh wrote about it?

*(Children of class nod. Minister reads p. 62, paragraph 4, and p. 63.
Youth group in love feast scene.)*

MINISTER: And that's the way it was. How fitting it was that those early
   Brethren chose our Lord's birthday as the birthday of our American church,
   for without Jesus we would have no church. If Jesus had not come to be our
   Savior and Lord, we would have no anniversary to celebrate. No doubt those
   early Brethren thought about this many times that day as they pledged themselves to try to live after the example of Jesus. You see, our story really
   began long before Germantown, long before Schwarzenau. It began nearly
   2000 years ago in a stable.

(Nativity Scene pantomime with the junior high group.)

BENEDICTION

A Christmas Tree Festival for a family night in the Church

by Helen Temple Sutherland

Significant values may be realized when the family works and worships, plays, and prays, shares and sings together as suggested in this informal Christmas service.

Musical prelude: Christmas carols while families gather in the social rooms of the church.

Storyteller: Festivals are special events observed in a spirit of gaiety and goodwill. What greater festival is there in all the church year than the celebration of the birthday of him who came to bring love and life and joy? For this special occasion how fitting are trees, with arms pointing upward, dressed in green to speak of life and growth! Decked in glowing lights, sparkling brightly, they reflect happiness in friendly faces gathered here tonight. Would not Jesus like to know that we would celebrate his birthday with jollity, with stories dear, joyous carols, and gifts of love and cheer? In his name and for his sake we begin this family festival of decking the Christmas tree.

Announcer: What festive atmosphere can be wrought for Christmas by decking the halls with greens and bells and glowing candles! Bring them now while we sing. *(Young married couples deck the mantel, windows, piano, with greens, candles, bells or ribbons. Pianist continues to play until this activity is completed. In order to keep the program moving smoothly, the pianist will follow this procedure for each activity period in the service.)*

All sing: "Deck the Halls" (Old Welsh Air) Stanzas 1 and 2.

Storyteller: Legend of the Christmas Tree.

There is a legend that comes to us from early days of Christianity in England. Wilfred, a monk, was helping to spread Christianity among the Druids. One day, surrounded by a group of his converts, he struck down a huge oak tree. In the Druid religion the oak tree was an object of worship. As the tree fell to the earth it split into four pieces. From its center there grew a young fir tree, pointing a green spire toward the sky. The crowd gazed in amazement.

Wilfred let his axe drop and turned to speak. "This little tree shall be your holy tree tonight. It is the wood of peace, for your houses are built of the fir. It is the sign of an endless life, for its leaves are ever green. See how it points toward the heavens.

37

Let this be called the tree of the Christ Child. Gather about it, not in the wilderness, but in your homes. There it will be surrounded with loving gifts and rites of kindness.

Announcer: While the fir trees are brought and put in place, let us sing stanza one of "O Christmas Tree." *(During the singing of the carol young men bring the big and little trees and place them on either side of the room at the front.)*

All sing: "O Christmas Tree" (German Carol). Stanzas 1 and 2.

Storyteller: "The First Christmas Tree"

It is said that it was Martin Luther who actually had the first Christmas tree in his home. According to the story, he was walking through the pines and firs on Christmas eve. The stars shone so brightly upon the slender trees that they seemed to touch and light them. The sight was so beautiful that Luther cut a tree and took it home for his children. On the ends of the branches he fastened small candles and lighted them, so that the tree seemed to twinkle as though covered with stars. The children were delighted and happy with their Christmas tree.

Martin Luther wanted his children to remember Christmas as the birthday of the Christ Child, so he wrote the carol, "Away in a Manger," for them to sing.

Announcer: To deck our Christmas tree, bring lights that shine like the star in the winter sky, and let the children sing this much-loved carol.

(While the pianist plays this carol, young men place strings of lights on the big tree.)

Kindergarten and primary children sing: "Away in a Manger."

Announcer: In its natural setting in the out-of-doors the fir tree and pine are often bedecked with winter's most shining gifts of ice and snow. We too would have them upon our tree, so bring the make-believe snow and ice. *(While the pianist plays again "O Christmas Tree," young women bring icicles or snow spray to place on the tree, and arrange white cotton or cloth around the base of the tree. Appoint children to put some on the little tree.)*

All sing: "O Christmas Tree," stanza 3

Announcer: Wherever Christ is known, Christmas comes to all people, whether they live in cold or warm lands. In warm countries there are many beautifully colored fruits to make the day joyous and festive. Someone started the custom of make-believe fruit which we call tree ornaments.

(While the pianist plays carols softly family groups bring their tree decorations, placing them on the large tree. Under the guidance of a primary or kindergarten teacher the youngest children place their decorations on the little tree. Families come by groups, following the order of those whose last names begin with letters (1) A to C, (2) D to Q and R to Z, or more groups if the audience is large.)

38

All sing: "O Christmas Tree," stanza 4

Storyteller: Sometimes people are so busy keeping Christmas in their own ways that they almost forget about Jesus Christ. That was the way it seemed to Francis of Assisi long ago. To help the people feel their true love for Christ, he arranged a life-size nativity scene in a cave near his town. So it has become a custom to use a nativity scene, called the creche, at many times and places to help us remember Christ at Christmas.

Announcer: Bring now a part of the nativity scene and arrange it under the tree, as we listen to the Bible reading and a Christmas lullaby.

A Scripture reading: Luke 2: 4,5 and 7   *(By a young mother)*

(While the pianist plays the next carol, two children place the stable, manger, babe, Mary and Joseph under the large tree. Young men turn on the tree and creche lights.)

Solo: "What Child Is This?"   *(By a young woman)*

Announcer: Let us hear more of the beautiful Christmas story as told in the gospel of Luke and then add the shepherds to our nativity scene.

Choric speaking: Luke 2: 8-16   *(To be given by older primary or junior boys and girls under the direction of a teacher, or by the entire group under the leadership of the storyteller or song leader.)*

(During the reading of the last two verses, two children add the shepherds to the nativity scene.)

Juniors sing: "Angels We Have Heard On High."

Announcer: Now let us hear the story of the first Christmas gifts.

Choral reading: Matt. 2:1-10   *(To be given by juniors or junior high youth directed by a teacher or by the entire group guided by the storyteller or song leader.)*

Announcer: To remind us of that guiding star on the first Christmas bring now the star and place it on the top of the tree, while the men sing, "We Three Kings of Orient Are." *(A young man puts the star on the large tree.)*

Men sing: "We Three Kings of Orient Are," stanza 1

Storyteller: There is more to that story of the first Christmas. *(Reads Matt. 2:11.)*

Prayer of dedication of life

All sing: *(Remain standing, with only a spotlight on the Christmas tree and the creche.)*   "Silent Night."

PREPARATION FOR THE FESTIVAL

The preparation for this festival may have as many values, if not more, than
the actual service. Not hurried last minute preparation will achieve such
goals, but advanced, thorough planning. This will make it possible in the
Sunday school, other church sessions, and in the home, for all church people
to be participating, week by week, in learning activities and experiences
which may be shared joyfully at this Christmas festival.

The planning may be done by the Sunday school council or a committee appointed
by the Nurture Commission. This group may adjust the plans to meet the needs
of the local church. This committee will be responsible for the general planning, delegating work to the various groups within the church, and checking to
see that all groups are functioning and ready.

Plans will include: 1. The date and time; 2. Leaders and group participation;
3. Publicity; 4. Room arrangements and materials; 5. Sharing activities.

1. *The date and time.* If possible, allow two Sundays in December before the
festival so that the children's preparation may be a part of their learning
experiences in the church school. When small children are participating, an
afternoon service or early evening hour is desirable.

2. *Leaders and group participation.* A good pianist, song leader, girl soloist, an announcer, and a storyteller will be needed. The storyteller should
tell his part rather than read it. Suggestions for group participation include
young married people, men's and women's groups, youth fellowships, juniors,
primary and kindergarten children. Plan what each group will do for the
festival. Then, give their leader a copy of the entire program with directions
and responsibilities marked. Do this early enough that teachers can include
these plans in their teacher planning for December.

All groups should be ready to give their assigned program parts and to place
trees and decorations in a few minutes and with ease.

3. *Publicity.* Announce the festival two or three weeks before the planned
date. The week before the service, send a reminder similar to this:

*Before our Christmas tree festival, would your family
like to prepare tree decorations to bring to the church
to deck the tree on Christmas family night? If so, make
it a time of family fun and fellowship at home. Be
creative and original, using scrap materials or things
that are not costly. What can you create of beauty and
interest from cardboard tubes, can lids, aluminum foil,
points, paper cups, colored paper, string, ribbons,
popcorn, candied cereal, cookies, or old greeting cards?*

4. *Room arrangements and materials.* Use the social rooms of the church and
create an informal atmosphere by arranging the chairs in semi-circles facing
a fireplace.

On either side place a screen, in front of which the trees will be placed. The persons speaking for the trees in the dialogue will be hidden behind the screens. The announcer and storyteller may be seated at one side of the front near a reading stand. The song leader and pianist will be near the piano on the other side.

There will be needed a large tree and a two or three-foot tree, arranged on tree stands. Secure all materials for decorating and mimeograph the programs, including words of songs. If the choral arrangements of the Scriptures are to be given by the entire group, include them on the programs.

5. *Sharing activities*. The planning committee, after consulting with the pastor, may decide to deliver the tree (or trees) to shut-ins.

"Plan your work and work your plans" is a very good motto to follow to make this festival a happy experience for all the families of the church.

Hanging of the Greens in worship

Services of the "Hanging of the Greens" are sometimes held on the first Sunday of Advent. Lyle D. Roth used the following several Sundays preceding Christmas Sunday at South Bay Community Church of the Brethren, Redondo Beach, California. Notes Lyle, "I have used this service about eight times. It varies a little each year in movements and decorations and interpretation, but the general format is the same."

ORGAN PRELUDE

INVOCATION

HYMN   O Come, All Ye Faithful

CHRISTMAS LITURGY

Leader: Blessed be the Lord God of Israel; for he hath visited and redeemed his people.

People: *Thou art the King of glory, O Christ!*

Leader: Through the tender mercy of our God, the day spring from on high has visited us.

People: *Thou art the everlasting Son of the Father, O Christ!*

Leader: We thank thee, O God, for the birth of Jesus, that thy Spirit was upon him.

People: *For unto us a Child is born; unto us a Son is given.*

Leader: Help us, O God, to feel the weight of the world's sorrow and need, to be made aware of the power of evil, to see humankind's spiritual loss caused by hatred and sin.

People: *Cast out our sin, and enter in! Be born in us today.*

Leader: Forgive our insufficiency, our failure to respond to thy bidding; grant us courage to face the day with supreme confidence that we can do all things through the One who is our strength.

People: *May the light of the shining star that gives joy to all be in us, that we may be reborn to a life of new hope, and that we may be numbered with thy saints in glory everlasting.*

CHRISTMAS PRAYER AND HYMN   Angels We Have Heard on High

THE MEANING OF THE SERVICE   (Explained in later paragraphs)

THE PULPIT AND LECTERN GREENS...The Prophecy, Isa. 7:14; 11:1-5; 9:2-7.
   The Interpretation...The Presentation,   O Come, O Come, Immanuel

*Note: The scripture throughout is responsive reading, using two readers.
   The format for the presentation is the same for all sections except the
   Nativity. While the congregation sings, two young people place wreaths
   made of greens on the pulpit and lectern.*

THE INSTRUMENT AND CHOIR GREENS...The Scripture, Luke 2:8-15...The Interpretation, Matt. 2:1, 9b-11...The Presentation, Hark the Herald Angels Sing

THE SANCTUARY GREENS...The Scripture, Isa. 6:13, 41:19-20...The Interpretation...The Presentation, Deck the Halls

*Note: The decoration in this case includes a pre-decorated tree. All of
   the window sills in the sanctuary have been decorated with candles and
   some greens. In this case we added only holly. Two adult women decorate
   two windows.*

THE ALTAR GREENS...The Interpretation...The Presentation, As With Gladness
   Men of Old

*Note: Greens have been placed on the altar before the service along with
   the candle. All that is added is a cross made from greens carried and
   placed by two older men.*

THE LIGHTING CEREMONY...The Scripture, John 8:12; Matt. 5:14-16... The Interpretation...The Lighting, O Little Town of Bethlehem

*Note: While the choir sings, all the candles are lit in the windows, on the
   instruments and on the altar table. Use several candlelighters. The sanctuary is darkened for this and remains darkened for the Nativity.*

THE NATIVITY...The Scripture, Luke 2:4-8... The Interpretation...The Presentation, O Holy Night, by the Chancel Choir

*Note: We use the baptistry, which is in the center of the chancel area here.
   At other times I have used a table in the chancel area. Large figures are
   used; the white plastic ones for lawn use are good. Up to this point they
   have been covered or are behing a curtain. The choir sings O Holy Night,
   with a soloist singing the verses. When they get to "fall on your knees,"
   the choir comes in very strongly. At that precise moment a spotlight is
   turned on illuminating the nativity scene. Just Mary, Joseph, and the baby.*

THE DEDICATION...The Scripture, Matt. 2:10-11... The Offering, Joy to the World

Note: A word is said about sharing the joy of this season and the promise of Joy to the World. The benediction is actually the congregation singing as they leave the sanctuary.

THE MEANING OF THE SERVICE

GOD IS WITH US...Jesus has come! This message brings joy to all of the people of the world who hear and know. The promise has been fulfilled. The kingdom of God is here, is coming, and will continue to come. We need no longer wait for a Messiah, for he is already with us, and if we continue to wait and look, we deny the validity of the gift God has already given.

Many years ago a son was born to a happy couple. The delivery room and maternity ward was said to have been a barn. Not a deserted barn, not a converted barn, but an ordinary barn which the young family was called upon to share with the animals. It is a rather unlikely place for God to show how he wishes to enter into the everyday life and affairs of humanity, but that is the way that it did happen.

That is what happened. God chose a barn, a poor young couple unknown to the world, a time of unrest and upheaval, a time of riots and civil disorder, a time of poverty and discontent, a time of religious problems, a time that taxes were being paid, in fact a time whose description almost perfectly matches a description of our own times.

A baby boy named Jesus was born, that is true; and we celebrate that birth. But the real celebration that we are called to is the fact that we are not alone. God is with us, not just in the polished living rooms of our homes, or in the structures of our churches, or in some narrow confines of our life called the religious or spiritual side of life. When persons are drawn together in concern and justice, there is God's kingdom being acted out whether that is in a judge's chambers or in an altar call. Where persons are recognized as persons who are worthful, there is the appropriation of the Christmas message, whether that be in a federal prison or in a home. Wherever healing takes place, whether it be in a service of anointing or in a state mental institution there is God's presence being made real and visible.

The hymn, Where Cross the Crowded Ways of Life, best expresses this. (Read verses 1,2 and 6.)

The understanding of God's presence, casting new light on all our experiences, is certainly essential in our Christmas celebrations and decoration. Many of our customs of this season have pre-Christian and pagan beginnings. Many have been called into question because of this. Some scream idolatry, un-christian, materialism, and other rather well-chosen derogatory words.

But it is in this reality that the beauty of Jesus' birth comes sharply into focus. It is here that the power of Christianity comes into play. For as we have appropriated pre-Christian and pagan celebrations, we have transformed them and given them new significance.

God does not always form new institutions to inaugurate his kingdom. He does not always start new churches for his Word to be shared. Rather he most likely will continue to do as he has done, to speak the new in the midst of the old, the common, the everyday.

Therefore, this year, through this service, we hope to shed new light on some old customs, in the faith that it will make our family and church celebrations more significant. We want to make these festivities and decorations part of our corporate life in the church. The holly, the evergreen or pine boughs, the wreaths, the trees, and the lights and sounds of this season will be a part of our celebration.

We do not wish to draw you out of your life to a manger in a barn in Bethlemen, but rather to sharpen sensitivity to the presence of the truth of that manger in your life today. For it is there that the Kingdom of God in Christ came and will continue to come.

THE PULPIT AND LECTERN GREENS

The Scripture throughout the service is read responsively by two readers. Here is one proposal:

1. The Lord himself will give you a sign. Behold, a young woman shall conceive and bear a son and shall call his name Immanuel. Isa. 7:14.

2. *There shall come forth a shoot from the stump of Jesse, and a branch shall grow out of his roots. And the Spirit of the Lord shall rest upon him. Isa. 11:1-5*

1. The people who walked in darkness have seen a great light:

2. *Those who dwelt in a land of deep darkness, on them has light shined.*

1. Thou hast multiplied the nation, thou has increased its joy; they rejoice before thee

2. *As with joy at the harvest, as men rejoice when they divide the spoil.*

1. For the yoke of his burden and the staff for his shoulder, the rod of his oppressor, thou hast broken as on the day of Midian.

2. *For every boot of the tramping warrior in battle tumult and every garment rolled in blood will be burned as fuel for the fire.*

1. For to us a child is born, to us a son is given;

2. *And the government will be upon his shoulder,*

1. And his name will be called

2. *Wonderful Counselor*

1. Mighty God

2. *Everlasting Father*

1. Prince of Peace

2. *Of the increase of his government and of peace there will be no end.*

1 & 2. *The zeal of the Lord of hosts will do this. Isaiah 9:2-7*

45

THE INTERPRETATION

We have just heard some of the Biblical prophecies of ancient Israel which seem
to have been fulfilled in the advent of Jesus. These were the dreams of
great men of God with great wisdom and sensitivity. They looked forward
to a time when God would be with men and attempted to describe it.

Tonight as we look back, it is easy to say that not all of their words were
fulfilled in Jesus. However, if we do that we either discredit their
prophecy, or the fact that God is with us. The fondest dream of Isaiah
was that of God being with man. It would be a time of plenty, a time of
justice, a time of righteousness. Tonight let us not mourn the incomplete-
ness of plenty in our world, or the injustice that is present, or the un-
righteousness that we see. Rather, let us celebrate together God's presence
in the plenty that is here, in the justice that we experience, and in the
righteousness that is apparent. Let us not look so much forward to a time,
but look into our time and discover where God is.

That is the Word of God to us in the event of Jesus' birth. He is with us
in the ordinary dimensions of life, whether it be a barn or a temple.
That word continues to come to us from the pulpit and lectern in our sanctuary. God is with us. His kingdom is established. It is complete, but
we do not experience its completeness. It is total even though we miss
its totality.

So tonight we experience the call to recognize the Kingdom of God as we place
a wreath of greenery on the pulpit and lectern. It is a symbol to remind
us of the unchangingness of the kingdom by the use of the evergreen, the
wholeness of the kingdom by the full and complete circle, and its location
comes as a challenge to those who minister from it and to those who receive
a ministry from it to continue to seek out the kingdom and help it to be
born in the hearts and lives of all persons.

Let us give our attention to the hymn, O Come, O Come, Immanuel, paraphrased,
Come, God, open me to experience your kingdom.

THE INSTRUMENT AND CHOIR GREENS

According to one ancient account, a group of shepherds were huddled together
against the cold breeze of the night. They were only a few miles from the
little town of Bethlehem oblivious to all that was happening in the barn
below them. It was just another night, filled with the discomfort of the
plain, the constant fear of wild animals, sounds which made sleep shallow
and difficult, and the bone-chilling cold.

But suddenly, around them appeared a brilliance which blinded their sleep-
filled eyes. A terrible fear struck them, a panic developed that closed
their mouths. But then there was a voice, calming in its message, "Don't
be afraid, something wonderful has happened. God has come to you, and to
all, tonight, in a barn in Bethlehem."

Another account has three wise men from the East traveling for days to see a child. They were guided by a star, we were told. Astronomers have wrestled with this for centuries usually missing the beauty of the story. An everyday thing, a sign, a guide, a star, appeared and gave direction and meaning to these men's lives, and they gave the best they had in response.

Tonight we shall place a star of greenery over the choir and boughs of greenery on our musical instruments. Leadership and direction in worship are expected from both, but also the music of our church is disciplined and guided by the star. The message of Christmas is pin-pointed and drawn together by this star again tonight.

Hark, the Herald Angels Sing, is a favorite Christmas carol, full of joy and response, pointing to the spirit loosed by the fact that God is with us. The angel voices still sing, with many voices, and the star still guides with many shapes.

SANCTUARY GREENS

Very soon in our homes the Christmas tree will occupy a prominent place. Not only will it take up a lot of space, but as the gifts begin to appear under it, children and parents will spend some time there also. When the Christmas tree is set up and decorated, the Christmas season has arrived officially. The tree has become one of the central symbols of this season.

Doubt and criticism have been directed toward its use. Some say the tree is a pagan symbol and should have no place in our Christmas celebrations; it almost certainly has pre-Christian beginnings. Actually the Christmas tree has come under the mysterious changing power of the Christ event and has been transformed. It points to a truth of this season and helps us to express the joy and happiness of this time. What greater joy is there to celebrate than that the old has become new, the narrow has become all-emcompassing, the law has become freedom and love! And this is expressed in the Christmas tree. It is usually just an ordinary pine with misplaced and misshapen branches, but it becomes beautiful and is transformed by the decorations and the place it is given. The boughs of greenery too--scraps to some persons, to be cut up and thrown into the fireplace--can become things of beauty and symbols of life. They too transform an ordinary room into a place of celebration.

The joy of the experience of God with us is found in the carol, Deck the Halls. Let us express this joy now as we sing and receive the sanctuary greens.

THE ALTAR GREENS

As we enter the sanctuary to meditate and worship, the altar table stands as a point of focus, calling all our experience and life together and pin-pointing it in relation to our faith.

What greater symbols of the Christian faith are there than a candle and a cross? The candle in its whiteness suggests purity and wholeness. As it is lighted it speaks of warmth and understanding light.

Our faith has always centered around the cross. The vertical bar of the
cross is said to represent God in his relationship to all of mankind, the
horizontal bar to symbolize the relationships that are called for with our
fellow man. This evening the cross that we will place on our altar table
is a cross of greens. This is fitting also as the evergreen holds its col-
or and its life through all the seasons, in a way unchanging and certain.
How well this points to the love extended to us in the birth and gift of
Jesus to us, both then and now.

Let us meet each other now in God's presence as we are presented with the altar greens.

THE LIGHTING CEREMONY

Have you ever traveled across the country at night in an automobile? Often
in the great expanses of the plains and desert a light becomes most meaningful. When the gas gauge shows a tank less than ¼ full, or there is a
hollow feeling of hunger in the abdomen, or a loneliness in the heart, light
means fuel, food, and company.

The very basis of life is light. If it were not for light and its warmth,
life would be impossible, for light is needed for the process of growth.
The scriptures indicate that God with us in Christ is like light to us, a
necessity for true life. And the message of this season is that precisely.
He is here...giving light and life to daily living, joy to loving, satisfaction to eating, and meaning to existence.

There is a quality of warmth and intimacy in the light of a candle that has
never been equaled by technological creations. As we light the candles
this evening, may those in the windows represent an invitation to all who
are outside to participate with us in the warmth and concern found within.
As the candle on the altar is lit, let it represent to us the center of
our life and worship, the center of our celebration.

The lights on the Christmas tree transform a hulking shape into a thing of
sparkling beauty. How well that speaks of God's presence through Jesus
the Christ.

THE NATIVITY

The nativity scene is displayed all over the country and in many parts of the
world today. It is present in the midst of both great wealth and utter
poverty. Live persons and animals re-enact the story; expensive figures
or cheap ones made of paper depict the scene.

Tonight as a climax to our service we shall focus once more on that scene in
a barn in Bethlehem. But we should be aware of something beyond this baby
in a manger. Tonight let us recall the beginning of a life that was lived
for others, a life of purpose and certainty.

Jesus was certain about why he was here. At the age of twelve he was already
rather independent in purpose, and when he was called into question, he
made a very typical adolescent response--"Can't you understand I have something very important to do? I must be about my father's business."

But in that the tone was set for his life. It was twenty years later. His best friend was dying, the messenger said. Jesus responded, "I am very busy now--I will be there in a few days." His course was set, his purpose was clear. In another place it says that he set his face firmly toward Jerusalem. He knew what his task was, and that was to "be God with us." As we experience the nativity tonight, let us respond to the purpose of the life represented in that birth, respond to God made known to us, God present with us.

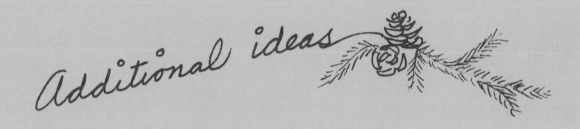

Additional ideas

Hanging of the Greens can take on the air of our heritage. Using gingham bows (lined with paper for stiffening) on wreaths, garlands and window arrangements.

Window arrangements can be made from pieces of plywood about 12" long and wide enough to fit on the window sill. Drive an 8 penny nail up through the center to fasten an 8" candle (see diagram). Add an old fashioned lamp chimney, greens that have been treated with floral *Clear Set* and bows of gingham.

Plan programming using Christmas carols sung without accompaniment and scriptures depicting the Christmas story.

Create you own Hanging of the Greens by combining ideas you have read or creating new ones.

Celebration Centers for Christmas

Celebration centers should be created from the content of worship. Following are ideas for developing visual centers which convey the scriptural message of the Christmas story. Remember to make centers large enough to be seen and understood from anywhere in the sanctuary.

Make a hanging by gluing straw to wallpaper or cheese cloth to be used as a backdrop for the manger. Add hanging candles in gallon jars. (Directions may be found in the section on candles.)

Create banners for each event of the Christmas story. Process during worship with the appropriate banner for use in the service. After worship, hang the banner on a side wall to make way for the second banner the next week. Continue this process until Christmas eve, when the last banner is placed in front, surrounded by all the banners telling the complete Christmas story.

Make a banner of long strips of felt. Each strip tells part of the Christmas story using simple forms and symbols. Add a strip to the pole each week if you wish.

The same banner could be hung on a circular rod which is suspended from the ceiling in the center of the sanctuary to be viewed from all sides.

Banners may be hung on side walls, front walls, suspended from the ceiling and displayed on flag poles in stands.

50

Design and make ceiling to floor wall
hangings using simple symbols or words
of Christmas. Repeat the pattern over
and over with silk screen method.

Hangings may be made of nylon net with large silhouettes of
felt glued on to represent near east landscapes or figures
depicting the nativity.

Hangings may also be made by tie-dying large pieces of cloth
a deep blue to resemble a starry sky.

A cradle and a shepherds crook, surrounded with straw
might be used. Light the cradle from behind or within.
Drape a blanket or cloth over the edge of the cradle on
Christmas eve.

The Jesse tree or Chrismons tree explained
in the Advent section of this book could
be used as a celebration center.

Fill a manger to over-flowing with all the trappings of a
commercial Christmas. Take away a certain number of the
commercial things each week until all that is left on Christmas
eve is a cradle, lighted from within and three simple gifts
at the foot.

Advent wreaths made larger can
be used for the sanctuary. They
may be hung, stood vertical
using lamp chimneys over
the candles, and may be made
of different things. See the
section of this book on the
Advent wreath for ideas.

A large mobile using symbols of the
Christmas story or birds made with
origami could be created as a visual
center.

51

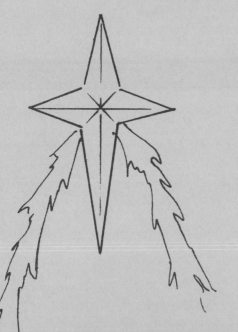

Begin with an empty setting backed with a
hanging of simple blue cloth. Each week
add a symbol representing a part of the
Christmas story. Examples are; a large
scroll with the prophecy, an empty manger or
cradle, a shepherd's crook, a large hanging
candle or a lighted star, and three gifts.
These could be brought forward by children
during the worship service or placed by the
environment committee prior to the service
each week.

Make a large simple star with a wood frame. Laminate the
frame with thin cloth that has been waxed and colored in
batik fashion using shades of yellow and white. Light from
behind. Hang the star very high and suspend two ropes of
greens from the star similar to the drawing. Leave floor
space open for live drama or place very simple objects that
express the theme.

Ideas presented in the section of this book
on the creche could be enlarged and used as
a celebration center.

Create a 5 pointed star of wooden
strips, 24" in length. Fasten it to
a wooden base. Use 3 white candles to
symbolize the three wise men. Place the
objects on a deep blue cloth which
has been draped over the communion
table. If you wish, you may begin
the service using just the cloth
and candles. Have a child bring
the star and place it on the
center as part of the children's
story, before or after the scripture
is read. This center would be appropriate for Epiphany.

The Songs of Christmas

The Songs of Christmas

Singing has been a joyful expression
for people everywhere. Whatever we may
have experienced can give rise to a tune in
our hearts. So it has been with the story of
Christmas. Persons from the early days of Christen-
dom have created music to give thanks for this most
precious gift of God.

The first chants, hymns, and litanies in Latin were likely too theological for
the common person to sing. During the thirteenth century, under the influence
of Francis of Assisi, carols were written in a language people could understand
and in the words that the common person used. A carol is a religious song
treated in a festive, familiar manner. The songs passed from Italy to France
and Germany and soon to England, everywhere retaining their simplicity, devotion, and joy.

The custom of the star singers as told in Betty Nickerson's "Celebrate the
Sun," was once widespread in Europe. Singers traveled through the wintry night
bearing a huge lantern in the shape of a star, stopping outside homes in many
lands to sing.

In countries including Sweden, Switzerland, Austria, the Netherlands, during
the time between Christmas eve and Twelfth night, one might hear the sound of
singing echo across the frozen land. Singers often dressed in costumes to
represent the Three Kings, with crowns of gold paper and robes of regal design.
Their leader would carry the star of Bethlehem to light the way.

In Sweden the star boy would appear on January 6 to commemorate the arrival
of the Magi. Traditionally the star kings represented the three known divisions
of the ancient world: Europe, Africa and Asia. Consequently one member of the
trio would be black. Many times a group of costumed persons accompanied the
kings. One of this number often portrayed Judas who collected the gifts of
food or coins for celebrating the end of the caroling excursion. Singers were
often given sweets or something to drink to warm them on their travels.

The custom of the star boy seems to have evolved from the Nativity plays of
the Middle Ages when costumed troups of players traveled from town to town
presenting pageants. These traveling players helped to spread the story of
Christmas to persons who could neither read nor write. These early messengers of
song and story were welcomed as a special blessing to each home. If the singers
drew the initials of the kings and three crosses when they left the house, it
was believed that the year to come would have good furtune and freedom from harm.

54

The advance of literacy, television and theater may have taken over the educational function of these traveling minstrels, but the custom of carol singing lingers on. Most often it represents a time of good fellowship and fun. Occasionally it is combined with a collection for charity. No matter what the reason, the sound of voices raised in song on the crest of a winter night, is beautiful.

We are still creating the "joyful noise" of Christmas, we hope you will consider singing the new songs printed here along with many old favorites of your heritage. Sing the song of Christmas!

Resources adapted from "Celebrate the Sun" by Betty Nickerson (Lippincott, 1969)

Christmas Notes

A family or church party can rejoice in song. Learn new carols from the ones printed here, and sing some old ones too.

Cut from heavy cardboard and use as guide to cut cookies from dough with a sharp knife

Become familiar with tunes by having them played on the piano, guitar, or any instrument you might have. Then hum the tunes through. The next step is to "line" the words in the old fashioned Brethren way.

It is fun and interesting to relate some information about the origin of the familiar carols that we sing.

If you have soloists and ensembles, alternate them with congregationsl singing. Groups may be divided in many ways, children singing some, youth, older men and women, divided any way you wish.

A fellowship time for everyone following the sing, with note cookies and hot spiced punch.

Quick Crisp Sugar Cookies

Sift together into large mixer bowl:

4½ c. flour   2 tsp. baking powder
1 tsp. soda   1 tsp. salt

Add:

1 c. soft butter   4 eggs
      or margarine   2 c. sugar
2 tbs. milk   2 tsp vanilla

Beat with mixer until well blended.
Chill 2 hrs. Roll out on floured board
to 1/8" thickness, cut and bake at 400° F.
8 to 10 minutes. Sprinkle with colored
sugar before baking if you wish or frost
with powdered sugar frosting and decorate.

Whole notes can be cut with juice cans

Apple-Honey Tea

1 12oz. can frozen apple cider
            concentrate
2 tbs. instant tea
1 tbs. honey
½ tsp. ground cinnamon

In medium saucepan, reconsti-
tute apple cider according to
package directions. Add instant
tea, honey and cinnamon. Stir
to blend; heat through.
Makes 1½ qts.

Bar cookies decorated with a pastry tube

Frosted Molasses Creams

(two jelly roll pans full)

Measure into bowl:

4 c. flour   ¼ tsp. salt
2 tsp. cinnamon   ½ tsp. ginger
2 tsp. soda

Place in blender container:

1 c. molasses   1 c. shortening
2 eggs   1 c. sugar
1 c. warm water

Blend smooth and pour over dry ingredients. Mix well. Turn into two jelly
roll pans (10½ by 15½"). Bake 15 to 20
minutes at 350° F. Cool and frost with
powdered sugar icing. Cut into bars
and decorate with decorator tube to
resemble music staffs if you wish.

Hot Spiced Grape Punch

6 c. water
1 qt. grape juice
1 c. sugar
1 6oz. can frozen lemonade
1 6oz. can frozen orange juice
4 inches stick cinnamon, broken
6 whole cloves

Tie spices in cheesecloth bag
and add to rest of ingredients
in large sauce pan. Simmer 15
minutes. Remove spices before
serving. Serve hot. Makes 2½ qts.

Lemon-orange Icing

Place in blender container:
    2" sq. piece of orange rind
    2" sq. piece of lemon rind
2 tbs. orange juice   2 tbs. lemon juice

3 tbs. soft butter   1 egg yolk   dash salt

Blend until smooth and gradually add 3 c. confectioners' sugar. Spread on
molasses creams.

An Old English Caroling Party

Plan an evening of caroling
to friends and neighbors. It's
especially meaningful if you can
plan to visit and carol to nearby
nursing centers or retirement homes. Then
come back to church or home for a plum pudding
party, of hot plum pudding, rosy wassail, spiced
cider tea, and/or coffee.

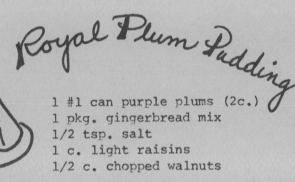

Royal Plum Pudding

1 #1 can purple plums (2c.)
1 pkg. gingerbread mix
1/2 tsp. salt
1 c. light raisins
1/2 c. chopped walnuts

Drain plums, remove pits and cut plums
in pieces. Prepare gingerbread mix
according to directions on package,
adding salt and plum pieces. Stir
in raisins and walnuts. Pour into
well greased 6 c. mold. Bake
uncovered at 375° F. about 1 hour.
Loosen edges and immediately
unmold on a serving plate.

-Jeanette Lahman

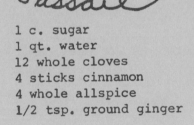

Wassail

1 c. sugar
1 qt. water
12 whole cloves
4 sticks cinnamon
4 whole allspice
1/2 tsp. ground ginger

Bring to a boil, add:

3 c. orange juice
2 c. lemonade
2 qt. apple cider or
   apple HI-C drink

Serve hot. Serves 18.

Twelve Days of Christmas

Text and tune by Kenneth I. Morse   Harmonization by Wilbur E. Brumbaugh

1. On the first day of Christ - mas God gives us all a
2. On the second day of Christ - mas God sor - rows at our
3. On the third day of Christ - mas God lifts a flam - ing
4. On the fourth day of Christ - mas The heav - ens burn with
5. On the fifth day of Christ - mas The skies break in - to
6. On the sixth day of Christ - mas God wraps the earth in

Child,   A ba - by, a broth - er, A
strife.   The mar - vel, the won - der, He
star   That all men should seek him Who
light.   No shad - ow, no dark - ness Can
song.   Such sing - ing, such mu - sic Al-
joy.   Come shep - herds, come sag - es To

friend both meek and mild.   A ba - by, A
turns our death to life.   The mar - vel, the
finds them where they are.   That all men should
turn that day to night.   No shad - ow, no
lows no place for wrong.   Such sing - ing, such
hon - or Ma - ry's boy.   Come shep - herds, come

broth - er, A friend both meek and mild._____
won - der, He turns our death to life._____
seek him Who finds them where they are._____
dark - ness Can turn that day to night._____
mu - sic Al - lows no place for wrong._____
sag - es To hon - or Ma - ry's boy._____

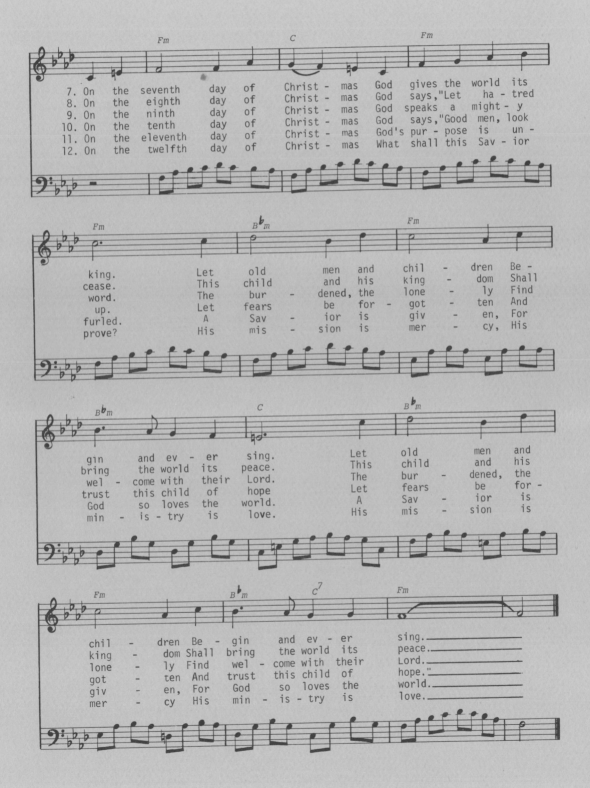

Have You Heard the News?

Music and words by Betty White

(1)Have you heard the news?(2)Have you heard the news?(all)This mar-vel-ous morn?(1)Have you

heard the news?(2)Have you heard the news? (all) A Sav-ior is born! (1) Have you

seen him yet?(2)Have you seen him yet?   (all) He's not ve-ry far! (1) Have you

seen him yet?(2)Have you seen him yet?(all) Just fol-low his star!_____ Just fol-low his

star!_____ Just fol-low his star!_____ Just fol-low his star!

A Christmas Lullaby

Music and words by Margaret Brown

1. Ba - by Je - sus sweet and small, Born in a
2. Sleep, sleep, Je - sus, close your eyes, Ma - ry and
3. Praise and hon - or to the King. Shep herds and
4. Born of Mar - y, vir - gin birth. Born___ to

low - ly cat - tle stall, With___ no pil - low
Jo - seph watch near by. An - gels guard___ your
wise men both did sing. Son___ of God,___ this
bring us peace on earth. Wel - come, Christ - child,

for___ your head And a man - ger for___ your bed.
head___ and feet. Close your eyes in peace - ful sleep.
Christ-child was born On that ear - ly Christ - mas morn.
on___ this day, Come in - to our hearts___ to stay.

Innkeeper

Steve Engle

Steve Engle

1. Inn-keep-er, Inn-keep-er, take me in, I'm so__ deep-down
2. Inn-keep-er, Inn-keep-er, don't you hear? Some-where a child is

wea - ry. Seen too__ much in the time I've been.
cry - ing. How ma-ny lost souls__ have been here?

Got an aw-ful load to car - ry. In-side your lights seem
Whom__ have you left for dy - ing.

cheer-y and warm! In-side there's food and laugh - ter!

Out-side the whole world's rag-ged and torn! Peace of mind's all I'm

af - ter. Inn-keep-er, Inn-keep-er, take me in,

I'm so deep-down wea - ry. Seen too__ much in the

time I've been. Got an aw-ful load to car - ry.

This Is Christmas Morn

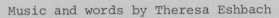

Music and words by Theresa Eshbach

If Stars Were to Sing

(a Christmas lullaby)

Kenneth I. Morse

Dianne H. Rist

1. If stars were like angels, this night would sing, if stars were like angels; If stars were to sing the heavens would ring, if stars were like angels. O child of my pain, O love of my

2. If stars were to sing and welcome a king, if stars were to sing, (to sing,) My child is the king whose praises they'd bring, if stars were to sing, (to sing.) O babe in a manger, child of my

heart,— O life of my own— life - giv - ing,—
dreams,— so frag - ile, so ten - der now sleep - ing,—

You are the— mu - sic, and you are the joy to make— each
You are the— prom - ise, and you are the sign that heav - en its

day— worth liv - ing. 3. If stars were like—
watch— is keep - ing.

an - gels, if stars were to sing, they would glo - ri - fy God and

wel - come their king, If stars were to sing-- then sing!

Why Is The Night So Still?

Kenneth I. Morse

Wilbur E. Brumbaugh

1. Why is the night so still, so holy?
   Why have the shepherds come to town?
   They come to see a child born lowly
   Here in a manger bedded down.

2. Why is one star so white, so radiant?
   Why are the skies ablaze with light?
   It is because the child of Mary
   Rests in the arms of God tonight.

3. Why do the heavens fill with music?
   What do these angel voices tell?
   They sing of Christ, the world's redeemer.
   God in our midst, Immanuel.

66

A Mary Carol

Ronald R. Hanft

Ronald P. Hanft

Moderately Slow

1. Mar-y said, Where will he lay his head? He'll nev-er own his bed And by the birds be fed. Mar-y said.
2. Mar-y cried, Who will be by his side? His friends will run to hide. Hang-ing a - lone, he'll die. Mar-y cried.
3. Mar-y smiled, Life will not be de-filed. His love is strength though mild. Lu - lay thou lit-tle child. Mar-y smiled.

1 & 2

3 rit.

Oo

rit.

67

This Child Is Alive

Music and words by Greg Bachman

Briskly

1. This Child is a - live, Born real in this world. He feels, eats and
2. This Child is a - live, Flesh, blood, eyes and bones. His life finds a
3. This Child is a - live, Born now in this place, Tran - scend-ing this

breathes In that straw where he's curled. He will grow to man-hood, He
home In ce - ment, steel and stone. He is streams and flow-ers, He
time, Serv-ing all by his race. If just for one hour___ His

will know bad from good. And when he's ma - ture He'll call for us
is gleam-ing tow-ers. He is how we see. This Child has a
in - fi - nite pow - er Were born ev-ery-where-- What change! Car-ing

to be his dis - ci - ples. Pure tho' we are not, We're glad for what
way of free-ing all good. We can't re-press him When all things ex-
sane-ly for each oth - er. Who can i - mag-ine the world to be

he's got. His life pulls us to life Be - yond our own.___
press him. His form molds our good-ness, His strength our love.___
fash-ioned When we bear the same love that's born by him!

From "The Christmas Window," Copyright © 1972 by Greg Bachman

A hymn for Advent

by Kenneth I. Morse

Too long this year has hid from sight
Its promise of that morning light
Which can dissolve the darkest night.

    O come, O come, Immanuel.

At last the time of hope draws near,
The dawning of a day so clear
That timid hearts may lose their fear

    And welcome thee, Immanuel.

Lord, grant that our awaking eyes
Reflect the radiance of thy skies
And turn from sleep to glad surprise.

    O come to us, Immanuel.

Lord, hatreds burden us with pain;
This anguished world must hear again
The shout of peace, good will to men

    O come once more, Immanuel.

*(to be sung to such tunes as numbers 40, 117,
186, 389 in THE BRETHREN HYMNAL)*

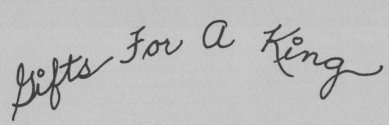

Gifts For A King

Kenneth I. Morse

Wilbur E. Brumbaugh

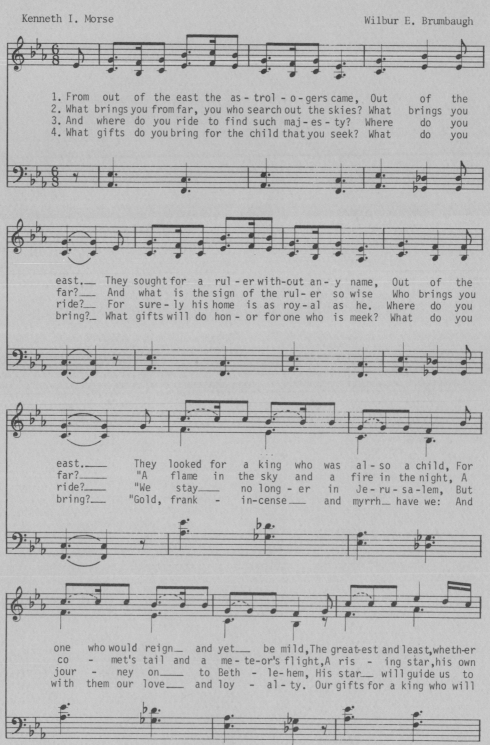

1. From out of the east the as-trol-o-gers came, Out of the east.__ They sought for a rul-er with-out an-y name, Out of the east.__ They looked for a king who was al-so a child, For one who would reign__ and yet__ be mild, The great-est and least, wheth-er

2. What brings you from far, you who search out the skies? What brings you far?__ And what is the sign of the rul-er so wise Who brings you far?__ "A flame in the sky and a fire in the night, A co-met's tail and a me-te-or's flight, A ris-ing star, his own

3. And where do you ride to find such maj-es-ty? Where do you ride?__ For sure-ly his home is as roy-al as he. Where do you ride?__ "We stay__ no long-er in Je-ru-sa-lem, But jour-ney on__ to Beth-le-hem, His star__ will guide us to

4. What gifts do you bring for the child that you seek? What do you bring?__ What gifts will do hon-or for one who is meek? What do you bring?__ "Gold, frank-in-cense__ and myrrh__ have we: And with them our love__ and loy-al-ty. Our gifts for a king who will

king   or child,   great-est and   least.
star so bright,   His   ris-ing   star."
find his home,   His   star will guide."
set   us free,   gifts for a   king."   "gifts for a   king."

There's Good News For You

Kenneth I. Morse   Wilbur E. Brumbaugh

Refrain: F   Bb   F   Dm   Gm   C7   F   Bb

There's good   news   for   you, good   news,_ good_ news for

F   Bb   F   C7   F   F   Bb   F   Dm

you   and   all   the world.There's a   time of   joy,great joy,

Gm   C7   F   Bb   F   Bb   C7   F   Fine

_ great_ joy! great   joy   for   all   the   world._

(C7)   F   Bb   F   G7   C7

1. Don't be   scared,you   shep-herds, God_ has heard you pray-ing, Lis-ten
2. Hear   the song of   glo-ry,   Sung_ from high-est heav-en For the
3. You   can cease your cry-ing. War-fare will be   end-ing.Peace on
4. He's   a   child for   hold-ing. He's_ a   star for guid-ing. He's the

F   Dm7   G7   C7   ⌢   (Refrain)

to   the   an-gels. Hear_ what they are   say-ing:There's good
ba - by   Je-sus, Who_   to earth is   giv-en. There's good
earth is   pro-mised. God_ his Son is   send-ing.There's good
hope you   long for. He_   is love a - bid-ing.There's good

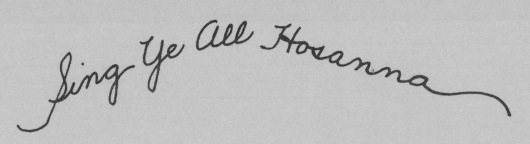

Sing Ye All Hosanna

Music and words by Steve Engle

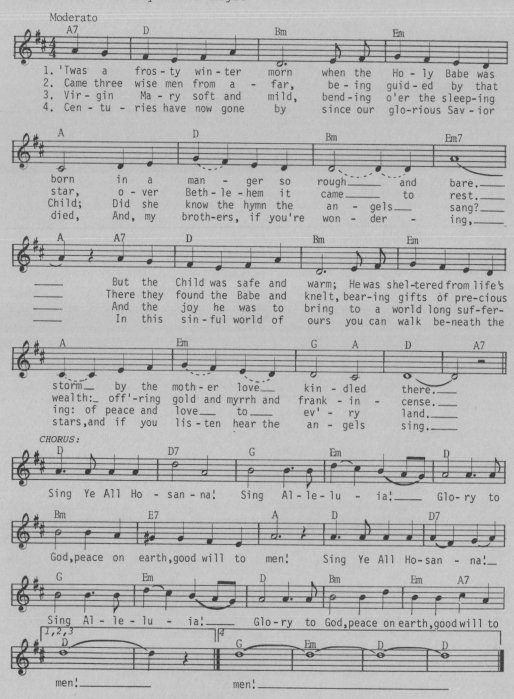

72

A Christmas Hymn Collage

Come, Thou long-expected Jesus,
  Born to set Thy people free,
From our fears and sins release us,
  Let us find our rest in Thee!
Israel's strength and consolation,
  Hope of all the earth Thou art,
Dear desire of every nation,
  Joy of every longing heart.

Come to Bethlehem and see
  Him whose birth the angels sing;
Come, adore on bended knee
  Christ, the Lord, the newborn King.
See Him in a manger laid
  Whom the angels praise above;
Mary, Joseph, lend your aid,
  While we raise our hearts in love.

Love Divine, all loves excelling,
  Joy of heaven, to earth come down:
Fix in us Thy humble dwelling,
  All Thy faithful mercies crown.
Jesus, Thou art all compassion,
  Pure, unbounded love Thou art;
Visit us with Thy salvation,
  Enter every trembling heart.

Yea, Amen! Let all adore Thee,
  High on Thine eternal throne;
Savior, take the power and glory,
  Claim the kingdom for Thine own:
Alleluia! Alleluia!
  God appears on earth to reign!
Alleluia! Alleluia!
  God appears on earth to reign!

(Sing to tune: "All the Way," No. 434, The Brethren Hymnal)

(The texts are from hymns 104, 138, 178, and 212, The Brethren Hymnal)

arr. by Wilbur E. Brumbaugh

Carols To Create

Here are two simple carols, one of which is a round, composed by Steve Engle. Steve did not write lyrics for these tunes. That is up to you! Begin by playing or humming the tunes. You'll soon sense their rhythms and define their moods. Musicians and lyricists can create rhythmic gifts of their own in response to the Gift. And even if many of us have never written a tune or a lyric, a song can be a sign of love we'd want to try.

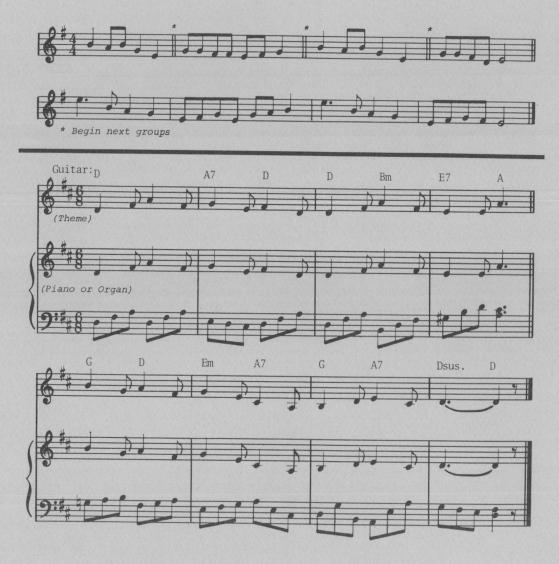

*Begin next groups

74

Prayers Litanies, Invocations for Christmas

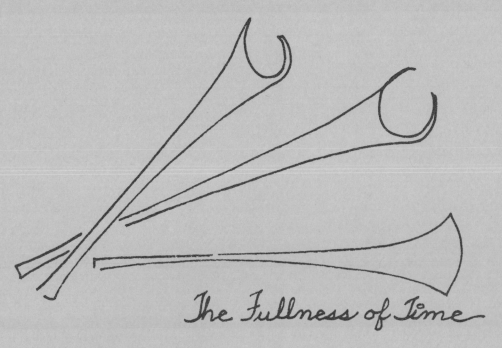

The Fullness of Time

Lord,

This is the season for the pure in heart:
Their songs of joy fill the air with music.

This is the time for the merciful:
Their deeds of kindness speak of goodwill to everyone.

This is the season for peacemakers:
Their trumpets sound the coming of the Prince of Peace.

This is the time for the bearers of glad tidings:
Their good news signals renewed hope for confused people.

Lord,

This is the fullness of time we have waited for.
A time for everyone, in every place, in every circumstance.

May joy, kindness, peace, and hope be ours
In this, Your season. Amen.

                    -Wilbur E. Brumbaugh

An Advent prayer

God, as Christmas approaches, we get mixed signals.
Make straight. Prepare ye. Decorate ye. Buy ye.
Give and send ye, and it shall be returned to you again.
Repent. Bow the head and bend the knee.

There are rough places on the Christmas card list, and
a valley in the checkbook where a hill should be. The
neighbors have made it plain that we need outdoor lights
and all the kids will make straight the highway to our
house. Cleanse ye the floors. Prepare ye the food.
We'd like to simplify our wants and review our motives
and priorities, but. . .

We are forever building up and tearing down, decorating and
throwing away, making up and washing off, fluffing up and
smoothing over, curling and then straightening, constantly
busy yet always unprepared.

It's no easier now than it was then. Fit for a king, and the
guest-of-honor is a beggar boy. Camped out in the barn, and
who should appear but royalty. Settled comfortably in our
tradition and this hairy man shows up shouting, "On your
knees! Bow down to this whoever-he-is!"

Help us to sort it all out, and give us your Messiah...anyway.

-Alan Kieffaber

Again

So he was born, now what?

So now he lives.

So shepherds spread the word, now what?

So the humblest of us are his messengers.

So wise men came, now what?

*So the wisest and mightiest kings, presidents, generals, and senators
must now know Christ is Lord of all.*

-Ronald K. Morgan

An Advent Call to Worship

Surely God is here. Now. In this place.
Let us recognize God's presence.
Let us recognize ourselves in God's presence.

So many changes come. Here. In this time.

Day after day the old familiar patterns yield to strange ways. There is always something new, something different, disturbing, challenging, upsetting.

So many changes come. And then they too pass away, like grass in the field that is first green, then gray, then brown, before finally it withers.

Or like a flower that buds, then blossoms in radiant splendor, before its petals fall away, and it dies.

Yet God does not change. The grass withers, the flower fades, but the word of our God will stand forever.

Surely God is here. Now. In this place.
This calls for a celebration.
Let it begin here and now.

An Advent Invocation

Come, eternal Spirit, come.
Come, with words of comfort and speak tenderly to us.
Come with reassurance and rekindle the fires of our faith.

We are among those whose longing hearts have yearned for a time when war shall be no more, when the mighty will be brought low, and the lowly will be lifted up, when a new king and a new kingdom shall guide us into the ways of peace.
Has not the mouth of the Lord so spoken? Will not the glory of the Lord be revealed so that all flesh, including our own eyes, shall see it together?

Eternal God, we do indeed look for that day, when the blind see, and the lame walk, and the stranger becomes a brother or sister, and everyone shall join in our cry, that God is with us.

O come, Lord Jesus, come. Thy kingdom come.
O come, O come, Immanuel. Amen.

-Kenneth I. Morse

How Silently the Wondrous Gift is Given

ONE: In the stillness of the night
        You came to people in ancient times
      while a town slept.

ALL: Only a few shepherds
        and some wandering star gazers
      found the baby in the straw.

ONE: Even the host for the night-the innkeeper-
        was unaware
          of the history-shaping event taking place
        in his cow stall.

ALL: And to us, You come...
            often quietly,
          unexpectedly,
        without fanfare,
      away from the noise and press of crowds.

                              -C. Wayne Zunkel

A Litany of the Inn

One: No room was the answer of the
      innkeeper so many, many years ago.

All: But let there be room for Him
      in the offices where we work and
      in the halls of our government.

One: No room was the answer of the
      innkeeper so many years ago.

All: But let there be room for Him in
      our homes, room for Him in our
      hearts, room for His peace, room
      for His love.

One: Asks the Lord, "Is there room for
      Me in your heart, or is it full
      like the innkeeper's inn?"

All: Lord Jesus, come into our homes,
      into our hearts, into our lives.
      There is room, Lord Jesus, there
      is room.

                              -Joseph Quesenberry

A Christmas Confession

(May be read in unison, by individuals, or responsively)

We were heavy with sorrow, but joy interrupted.
We were deep in the night, but a star appeared.
We were silent with sadness, but the heavens rang.

> *And the splendor shone around them*
> *When the time had fully come.*

We were hardened by conflict, but love intervened.
We were frightened by shadows, but light took them away.
We were haunted by fears, but a child brought us hope.

> *And she laid him in a manger*
> *When the time had fully come.*

We were dismal and defeated, but faith set us on fire.
We were weary and complaining, but our hearts discovered praise.
We were doubtful and confused, but a door to life was opened.

> *And the guiding star went before them*
> *When the time had fully come.*

We were arrogant and angry, but his innocence disarmed us.
We were cruel, crude, and clumsy, but his grace made all things new.
We were selfish, narrow, greedy, but his joy we had to share.

> *And they offered him their treasured gifts*
> *When the time had fully come.*

We were sheep who had lost their way, but the shepherd knew our names.
We were strangers without a country, but our kingdom came to us.
We were children far from home, but God sent his Son to guide.

> *And the Word was flesh among us*
> *When the time had fully come.*

—Kenneth I. Morse

A Post Christmas Prayer

LEADER:
  Lord, we confess that much of our Christmas celebration has been that of
  perishable blessings. We thank you, however, for that which is imperishable
  in the midst of all that is perishable.

PEOPLE:
  We rejoice in the midst of torn and crumpled wrapping paper--for the love that
  has been shared in the giving of gifts.

LEADER:
  We rejoice in the midst of presents that will soon be worn out--for friendships
  and family ties which have been renewed and which will endure.

PEOPLE:
  We rejoice in the midst of dried and falling pine needles--for your fresh and
  undying love in our midst, made flesh in Jesus of Nazareth.

LEADER:
  May the light which goes on because Jesus has come, illumine the lives of each
  of us, Father.

PEOPLE:
  May it be said of us. Father, that we received Him, that we believed in His
  name, that we received power to become the children of God.

LEADER: Amen!

PEOPLE: Amen!

                              -Rick Gardner

Antiphonal Reflections: "Who Was He?"

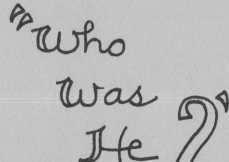

He was the Son of God.
    He was a human being.

He came down from heaven.
    He was born in a stable.

Kings came to his cradle.
    His first home was a cave.

He was born to be king.
    He was the child of Mary.

He was the greatest among leaders.
    He was the least among servants.

He was loved and honored.
    He was despised and rejected.

He was gentle and loving.
    He made many enemies.

He counseled perfection.
    He was the friend of sinners.

He was a joyful companion.
    He was a man of sorrows.

He said, "Rejoice."
    He said, "Repent."

He said, "Love God with all your heart."
    He said, "Love your neighbor as yourself."

He said, "Don't be anxious."
    He said, "Count the cost."

He said, "Deny yourself."
    He said, "Ask and receive."

In him was life.
    He died on the cross.

He was a historic person.
    He lives today.

He was Jesus of Nazareth.
    He is Christ the Lord.

—Kenneth I. Morse

That our roots might Flower

One: The Spirit of the Lord God is upon me, because the Lord has anointed me; he has sent me to bring good news to the humble.

ALL: Blessed are the meek, for they shall inherit the earth; and blessed are the poor in spirit, for theirs is the kingdom of heaven.

One: He has sent me to bind up the brokenhearted, and to comfort all who mourn; to give them garlands instead of ashes, oil of gladness instead of mourners' tears, a garment of splendor for the heavy heart.

ALL: Blessed are those who mourn, for they shall be comforted.

One: He has sent me to proclaim liberty to the captives and release to those in prison.

ALL: Blessed are those who are persecuted for righteousness' sake, for theirs is the kingdom of heaven. Blessed are you when men revile you and persecute you and utter all kinds of evil against you falsely on my account. Rejoice and be glad, for your reqard is great in heaven, for so men persecuted the prophets who were before you.

One: And everlasting joy shall be theirs. For the Lord loves justice and hates robbery and wrongdoing. He will grant them a sure reward and make an everlasting covenant with them.

ALL: Blessed are the merciful, for they shall obtain mercy.

One: Let me rejoice in the Lord with all my heart. Let me exult in my God; for he has robed me in salvation as a garment and clothed me in integrity as a cloak. For as the earth brings forth its shoots, so the Lord God will cause righteousness and praise to spring forth.

ALL: Blessed are those who hunger and thirst for righteousness, for they shall be satisfied, and great is their reward in heaven.

Barbara Kennedy

(Based on Isaiah 61:1-11 and Matthew 5:1-11)

The Word Became Flesh

Some do not understand,
"The Word became flesh and dwelt among us."
Most women understand explicitly
When a lover's words of devotion and promise
Become a factual pregnancy within us.

As the Word becomes increasingly flesh
Our bodies change,
Our lives change.
The Word takes shape within us,
And we are not the same!

Some forget it took nine months and Mary
For the Word to become flesh.
Untold ages of planning,
But even when God spoke
It took the usual nine to dwell among us.

Becoming flesh is a process - of love and labor -
Culminating with ecstatic pushings
Until the Word emerges
Amidst laughter and cries of joyous surprise,
Signaling it finally dwells among us!

The Word made flesh rearranges our worlds,
Our bodies,
Our homes;
Demands to be taken seriously;
Calls forth a response from us.

We who have given birth know what it means
For the Word to become flesh.
It happens to us
And we are not the same.
It happens to the world
And the world is not the same!

                              Mary Cline Detrick

Plays

Cantatas

86

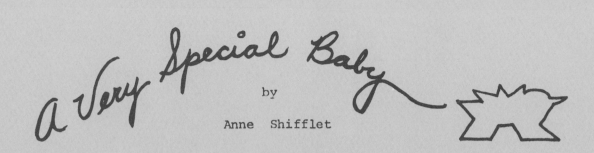

A Very Special Baby

by

Anne Shifflet

A VERY SPECIAL BABY is a dramatic interpretation of God's constant efforts to help his children learn to love and care for each other.

Since God always speaks in the present tense, it is suggested that all the actors, even those representing Biblical characters, dress in contemporary styles. The use of scenery and props is entirely optional.

Characters

NARRATOR

1st SOLOIST: arrogant, flashy dresser. Sings unaccompanied.

MOSES: the adult leader of a group of school children.

CHILDREN: speak, sing, and play rhythm instruments (optional)

HOSEA: outspoken, well-dressed.

AMOS: a farmer, dressed in work clothing.

MICAH: matter-of-fact, casually dressed.

2nd SOLOIST: sings with guitar in simple manner. Represents God's voice.

ISAIAH: authoritative, dressed in business suit.

JOSEPH: a tired, bedraggled young man.

INNKEEPER: the cordial host of a small, informal inn.

PETE: a boy working as a shepherd, dressed in rugged outdoor clothing.

JAKE: a boy working as a shepherd. He plays a recorder.

JOHN: a boy working as a shepherd.

ANGEL: voice and singing on prepared tape recording.

MARTHA: a young woman.

DORCAS: an acquaintance of Martha. They meet in the shopping center carrying grocery bags.

GIRL 1, GIRL 2, and GIRL 3: teenagers walking to school together.

MAN 1 and MAN 2: carrying attache cases, have just left their office for the

    day.

MAN and WOMAN: a well-dressed couple.

VOICE: represents Jesus speaking.

NARRATOR: God created the world and it was good.

   He made men to love and care for each other.
   He thought that people could get along, no matter whether they were rich
   or poor,
        old or young,
        black or white,
        brown or yellow,
        handsome or homely,
        parent or child,
        bright or dull,
        educated or unschooled,
        awkward or agile.
God just made every man, woman, boy, and girl to be his people.

   But somehow it didn't work out.
   Everyone seemed to care more for themselves than anyone else.

1st SOLOIST: (sings unaccompanied, in arrogant manner)

                        I Know What I Want

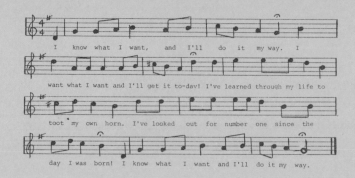

I know what I want, and I'll do it my way. I want what I want and I'll get it to-day! I've learned through my life to toot my own horn. I've looked out for number one since the day I was born! I know what I want and I'll do it my way.

   NARRATOR: And God wondered, "How can I help my people learn to love?"

           One time he got so angry he destroyed the world in a big
           flood, saving only Noah and the animals to make a fresh start.

88

But that didn't solve the problem, and God wondered, "How can I help my people learn to love?"

God talked to Moses and told him to write down Ten Commandments which would help people learn to love and care for each other.

(Moses is seated with a group of children around him.)

BOY: Weren't you scared when you talked to God, Moses?

MOSES: Well, maybe a little. But mostly I remember being excited. I was really excited about what he was telling me. Because I think these rules are going to work. Now let's see if you can remember the rules.

(Children pick up instruments and prepare to play.)

Ready . . . .

CHILDREN:

MOSES: We must worship nothing but God?

CHILDREN: That's right. No thing.

MOSES: No idols like animals?

CHILDREN: No birds. No fish.

MOSES: You must never bow to an image or worship it in any way.

89

GIRLS:

BOYS: You must <u>respect</u> God's name and not use it to swear.

GIRLS:

CHILDREN: *(speaking in rhythm)*

MOSES: On the seventh day?

CHILDREN: Rest.   *(draw it out slowly)*

MOSES: For God blessed the seventh day, and set it aside for rest.

(glockenspiel)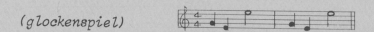

CHILDREN: Honor and respect your father and mother.

90

MOSES: That's a good way to keep a family happy.

(glockenspiel)

CHILDREN: You must <u>not</u> kill!   (drum)

You <u>must</u> be true to your own husband or wife.   (triangle)

You must not <u>steal</u> anything.

BOY: Not even a little thing.   (tambourine)

CHILREN: You must never tell a lie.

GIRL: Not even a little lie.   (finger cymbals)

MOSES: And last, but not least . . .

CHILDREN: Don't waste your time wishing you had other people's things.

MOSES: That's right. Be glad for what God has given <u>you</u>.

CHILDREN:

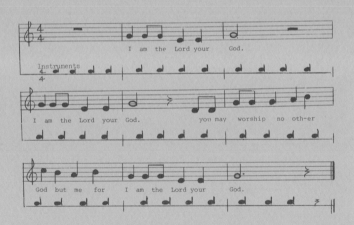

(Children place rhythm instruments where they can be picked up later.
The children are then seated in front pews.)

NARRATOR: But the people didn't remember to live by the rules. And God
wondered, "How can I help my people learn to love?"

God sent prophets to tell men how to live.

(Each prophet walks on to deliver his prophecy, then walks off.)

He sent Hosea . . .

HOSEA: The Lord has filed a lawsuit against you listing the following charges: There is no faithfulness, no kindness, no knowledge of God in your land. You swear and lie and kill and steal and commit adultery. There is violence everywhere, with one murder after another.

That is why your land is not producing: it is filled with sadness, and living things grow sick and die; the animals, the birds, and even the fish begin to disappear.

Don't point your finger at someone else, and try to pass the blame to him![1]

NARRATOR: He sent Amos . . .

AMOS: God hates your show and pretence - your hypocrisy of "honoring" him with your religious feasts and solemn assemblies.[2]

NARRATOR: . . . and Micah.

MICAH: He has told you what he wants, and this is all it is: to be fair and just and merciful, and to walk humbly with your God.[3]

NARRATOR: But the people wouldn't listen. They kept on caring for themselves more than anyone else.

1st SOLOIST: *(Repeat song "I know What I Want")*

NARRATOR: Then one day God had an idea. He would send his own son to live on earth and teach men how to live!

2nd SOLOIST:

I'll Send You a Baby

I'll send you a ba-by I'll send you a ba-by. I'll send you a ba-by, and he'll teach you how to live. Listen what he says when he talks to you; Watch what he does when he walks with you. I'll send you a ba-by, and he'll teach you how to live.

---

1   Hosea   4:1-4.
2   Amos   5:21.
3   Micah   6:8

NARRATOR: God's prophets began to tell people about God's plan. Isaiah tried to make them understand what God was going to do.

ISAIAH: I tell you: The Lord your God will be your everlasting light, and he will be your glory.

He has appointed one to bring good news to the suffering and afflicted. He will comfort the broken-hearted, announce liberty to the captives, and open the eyes of the blind.

The Spirit of the Lord shall rest upon him, the Spirit of wisdom, understanding, counsel and might; the Spirit of knowledge and of the fear of the Lord.

2nd SOLOIST: *(Repeat song "I'll Send You a Baby")*

NARRATOR: And then . . one night . . .

(The innkeeper is walking toward the stable door as Joseph appears from within.)

JOSEPH: It's a boy! And Mary seems to be doing O.K. I just thought I'd slip out for a minute to let you know everything is all right.

INNKEEPER: Well congratulations! And are you sure she's O.K.? I mean comfortable and all that? My, it's been a long time since me and my missus went through this. *(pauses, remembering)*

JOSEPH: Yea, would you believe, the manger!

INNKEEPER: *(laughing)* That oughta be right cozy. *(suddenly serious)* You don't know how bad I feel about this whole situation; me not having a decent place to put you up, with her due and all.

JOSEPH: Don't feel bad about that. You know how glad we were to find any place.

INNKEEPER: If they wouldn't have this stupid rule about everybody appearing in person for the census, we wouldn't have this overcrowding. Lord knows, I could use this business spread out a little.

JOSEPH: Yea, it does make it hard.

INNKEEPER: Just seems strange. Having a baby in a stable, and laying it in a manger.

JOSEPH: It is kind of strange. In fact this whole thing has been kind of strange . . . Oh well, don't want to get into that. But this is a very special baby.

Better get back in there. Just wanted to let you know.

INNKEEPER: Well, glad to hear. Goodnight.

(Joseph passes through the door into the stable. The innkeeper walks away.)

(Suggested congregational song: "Mary, Mary, What You Gonna Name That Baby?" by Richard K. Avery & Donald S. Marsh, or "O Little Town of Bethlehem."

(Three shepherds are seated on a hillside. Jake is playing a recorder.)

PETE: That's the sorriest sound I've heard in a long time. Jake, I wish you'd either practice when you're off duty or give up.

JAKE: I'm just trying to be a good shepherd. You know any well-qualified shepherd has to play the shepherd's flute. Even part-time shepherds. *(goes back back to playing recorder)*

PETE: *(After thinking about Jake's remark)*   Huh! Seems to me all you need to know for this job is how to stay awake all night.

JOHN: That's what Jake is trying to help you do.

PETE: Yea, sure.

(Turn on tape recorded sound of angels singing. Begin softly, gradually increase the volume as the shepherds speak.)

JOHN: Hush up, both of you. I hear something.

JAKE: Wow!

JOHN: What's going on?

PETE: Sh!

(The music continues briefly, then fades out and the angel's voice is heard on the tape.)

ANGEL: *(on tape)* Don't be afraid. I bring you the most joyful news ever announced. The Savior, yes, the Messiah, the Lord, has been born tonight in Bethlehem.

(pause on tape to allow shepherd's response)

JOHN: Down there? In Bethlehem?

PETE: You've gotta be kidding.

ANGEL: (on tape) No, it is true. If you go down there you can see him.
You will find the baby wrapped in a blanket, lying in a manger in the stable
behind Ishmael's Inn.

(music continues on tape, growing louder with "Glory to God in the Highest..."
then fades away)

JOHN: Come on, let's go. I know where Ishmael's Inn is.

JAKE: What about the sheep? We can't just leave them.

PETE: That's for sure. We'd all lose our jobs.

           Why don't you two go on? I think I can handle the sheep if you
don't stay too long.

JAKE: Would you? That's great.

JOHN: Come on. Let's go.

PETE: Go ahead.

(Jake and John leave their hillside and begin walking toward the stable
door in Bethlehem. Pete calls after them.)

           But you'd better tell me all about it when you get back!

JOHN: (shouting to Pete)   O.K.

JAKE: (When they are almost to the stable door) You know, I feel
kind of silly.

JOHN: I know what you mean. Do we just knock on the stable door and
say, "Pardon me, but may we see your baby? An angel told us you had one."?

JAKE: I guess. I want to find out what's so special about this baby.

(All three shepherds quietly walk off as narrator continues.)

NARRATOR: What was so special about that baby? It was God's own son, the
baby he had sent to teach men how to live.

           And that's what he did.

           Jesus healed the sick fed the hungry, counselled with the rich,
and helped the poor.

(Martha and Dorcas enter from opposite sides. They stop to speak as they meet.)

MARTHA: Hi! How are you?

DORCAS: Fine. How have you been?

MARTHA: O.K. And busy as usual. Say, have you heard about Joel?

DORCAS: Joel?

MARTHA: You remember, Joel, that deaf boy we went to school with?

DORCAS: Oh, yes. What about him?

MARTHA: He can hear! And he can speak clearly. That man Jesus that
   you've probably heard about was traveling through the town where Joel lives
   now, and Joel's friends talked him into going out to meet him. They wanted
   to see if Jesus would heal him like he's healed so many others.

DORCAS: And he did?

MARTHA: Yes. They say he wouldn't do it right in the crowd, but he
   took Joel into a courtyard away from the street for a few minutes, and
   when they came back, Joel could hear and speak!

DORCAS: That's wonderful! I wonder how Jesus does it.

MARTHA: I don't know. But what I keep hearing is that Jesus will help
   anybody, even people he doesn't know. They say he told Joel and his friends
   not to tell anybody about it.

DORCAS: Why do you think he did that?

MARTHA: I guess he just doesn't have time to heal everybody. But how
   could you not talk about such a miracle?

DORCAS: That's right. I want to tell James about this. I'd like for us
   to get to see Jesus sometime.

MARTHA: Yes, I'd like that too. Well, I'll see you later.

DORCAS: Nice talking with you. 'Bye now.

*(They walk off, continuing in the directions they entered. Three girls
enter from left. They talk as they cross front.)*

GIRL 1:   I don't believe it.

GIRL 2:   Nobody could do that.

GIRL 3:   But I saw it with my own eyes! Jesus said a prayer, then they
   started passing out the food, and there was more than enough for all those
   thousands of people!

(Girls exit to the right. Two men enter from right. They talk as they cross front.)

MAN 1:   I can go along with most of the things he's teaching, but that idea of "love your enemies" is too much. It goes against everything I've always believed about an eye for an eye and love your <u>neighbor</u>.

MAN 2:   I know. It's extreme. But it surely gives one something to think about.

(Men exit to the left. A man and woman walk down center aisle to front as narrator reads. They stand back to back in angry posture.)

NARRATOR: Jesus <u>showed</u> people how to live, and he <u>taught</u> people how to love.

VOICE: I have loved you even as the Father has loved me.

(Woman turns toward man in expectation. His back is toward her, and she turns back in disappointment.)

VOICE: When you obey me you are living in my love, just as I obey my father and live in his love.

(Man turns toward woman in expectation. Her back is toward him, and he turns away in disappointment.)

       I have told you this so that you will be filled with my joy. Yes your cup of joy will overflow!

(Both man and woman silently turn toward each other and embrace.)

       I <u>demand</u> that you love each other as much as I love you.

(Man and woman walk back center aisle hand in hand.)

NARRATOR: Glory to God, and peace on earth. . .

Peace on earth with every one loving and caring for each other,
no matter whether they are
        rich or poor,
        old or young,
        black or white,
        handsome or homely,
        parent or child,
        bright or dull,
        educated or unschooled,
        awkward or agile.
Every man, woman, boy, and girl living in love and peace.

Jesus said, "I am the way, the truth, and the life. No man cometh unto the father except by me."

And God said, "This is my beloved son in whom I am well pleased."

2nd SOLOIST:

I Sent You a Baby

(*Congregational Hymn: "Joy to the World." Children pick up rhythm instruments, stand in line across front, and play along during singing. Congregation stands, and remains standing for the benediction.*)

NARRATOR: Go, and love the Lord thy God with all thy heart, and thy neighbor as thyself. Amen.

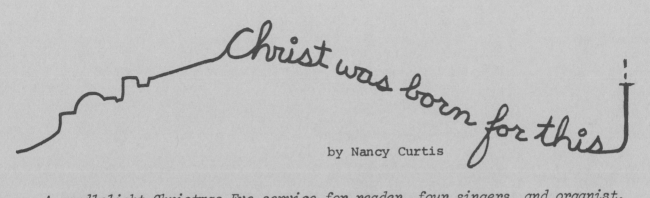

Christ was born for this

by Nancy Curtis

A candlelight Christmas Eve service for reader, four singers, and organist. This script originally was designed for a candlelight bread and cup communion service. You may wish to use it this way or to adapt it for some other purpose this Christmas season. The author is a member of the Nappanee, Indiana, congregation.

SINGERS: "Good Christian Men, Rejoice", verse 1.

READER: The setting is humble. The characters are humble. The incident could have gone unnoticed, for it is an oft-repeated, simple story. . . a father, a mother, a child brought into the world.

A child born on a night we never saw, in a land upon which we have never walked, in a stable of which we have learned from myths. There is no doctor. There is no nurse, There are no sterile gowns and instruments. There is no anethesia. There is a weary mother, an earthly guardian, and a Heavenly Father.

They tell us there was lowing of cattle. I tell you there was moaning from a mother's pain. They tell us there were no clothes for the child. I tell you there was a father's concern. They tell us it happens every day. I tell you a Heavenly Father looked down in love and hope on his creation and knew there could never be another night like it in all of history.

The mother is quiet now. It is over. There is no sound at all in the quiet night save the crying of the Holy Baby.

SINGERS: "Silent Night, Holy Night", verses 1 and 2

READER: A child born on a night we never saw, in a land upon which we have never walked, in a stable of which we have learned from myths.

There is no newspaper. There is no television. There are no Broadway plays or musical productions. There is no telephone. There are some shepherds and three wisemen and a star.

They tell us a brilliant light led to the place of birth. I tell you that the people were mystified and overcome, and that the awesome news of God's Son traveled by word of mouth faster than by teletype. They tell us that a king feared for his throne. I tell you that he had just cause to tremble in the wake of the greatest king of all. They tell us it was a natural phenomenon, a common curiosity that led the crowd to come and observe. I tell you there were voices from the heavens which rang out with "Glory Be to God."

The baby is quiet now. He is sleeping. There is no sound at all in the quiet night save the glorious harmony of angel voices.

SINGERS: "Angels, We Have Heard on High", verses 1 and 3.

READER: The setting is humble. The character is humble. The incident could have gone unnoticed, for it is an oft-repeated, simple story . . . a man kneeling in prayer.

A man kneeling on a night we never saw, in a land upon which we have never walked, in a garden of which we have heard from myths.

There is no minister. There is no priest. There is no congregation nor choir. There is no church. There is a man, and a lonely garden, and the spirit of God moving in their midst.

They tell us that he prayed all night. I tell you that courage for the ordeal ahead required meditation equal to a night of prayer for which none of us has the stamina. They tell us there was one who fell asleep. I tell you that One could have been one of us. They tell us that this man, God's Son, felt alone in his humanity unlike any of us have ever felt alone.

Christ is quiet now. He is praying. There is no sound at all in the lonely night save the heavy breathing of the one who was to watch.

SINGERS: "'Tis Midnight; and on Olive's Brow", verses 1 and 2.

READER: A man kneeling on a night we never saw, in a land upon which we have never walked, in an upper room of which we have learned from myths.

There is no set pattern of formality. There is no printed program. There is no fine music or beef prepared by the wives of deacons. There are no candelabra. There are a man, and twelve disciples, and a betrayer in their midst.

They tell us that Christ washed the feet of one follower. I tell you that this man knew the meaning of the word humility. They tell us this one incident set a precedent for churches far and wide. I tell you that Christ this night fashioned a symbol of his blood and body. They tell us that as often as we do this, we do it in remembrance of him. I tell you that Christ this night irrevocably linked us to himself, his manger, and his cross.

The disciples are quiet now. They are partaking of Christ. There is no sound at all in the upper room save the chewing of bread and the rasp of earthen mugs.

SINGERS: "According to Thy Gracious Word", verses 1 and 2.

(Reader or the minister will now administer the sacraments. Organ may play music throughout. Reader continues after the last person is served.)

READER: The setting is humble. The characters are humble. The incident could have gone unnoticed, for it is an oft-repeated, simple story. . . a man tried and executed for his crimes.

A man dying on a day we never saw, in a land upon which we have never walked, on a cross of which we have learned from myths.

There is no electric chair. There is no gas chamber. There is no brilliant lawyer for the defense. No jury paid in promises and bribes. There is no escape. There are a cross, and a Christ, and two thieves.

They tell us it was a mistake; he had done no wrong. I tell you that God gave up his only Son for the wrongs of you and me. They tell us that the story can be reexamined; that perhaps he was not dead at all. I tell you that the irrevocable truth is that God sent his Son into the world to perish this day, that we might understand his love. They tell us that God is dead. I tell you that Christ lives on.

Christ is quiet now. He is dying. There is no sound at all in this awesome day save the quaking of the earth when he utters, "It is finished."

SINGERS: "Were You There When They Crucified My Lord?", verse 1.

READER: A man resurrected on a day we never saw, in a land upon which we have never walked, from a tomb of which we have learned by myths.

There was no trick, There was no hypnosis. There was no artificial respiration or machine equipped for electronic breathing. There was no doubt. There was a risen Christ, an empty tomb, and a hope for us unlike any hope ever given to us before.

They tell us there is no life after death. I tell you this living Christ is proof positive, beyond a shadow of a doubt, that life for us does not end in the grave. They tell us these stories have little relevance to our busy, commercial, modern-day Christmas and Easter. I tell you that it is a long walk from a manger to a cross and that only a perfect man could manage the trail. They tell us that Christ is no longer in Christmas. I tell you, Christian friends, that without Christ there is no Christmas at all and that his birth and his death and his resurrection are for one holy purpose: that all might know for generations unending that God did so love the world that he sent his only Son.

SINGERS: "Good Christian Men, Rejoice", verse 3.

READER: And now it is Christmas. The setting is humble, the characters are humble. The incident could go unnoticed, for it is an oft-repeated, simple story . . . people gathered to worship.

People gathered on a day we *are* seeing, in a land upon which we *do* walk, in a church filled with unrest because of turmoils of which we learn from modern-day myths. There is no ceasing of strife. There is no complete peace. There is violence, countries torn by dissenters.

They tell us the best course is to press toward victory. I tell you that there is victory only in Bethlelem's baby. They tell us we cannot lose face. I tell you that we have lost face with the suffering peoples of the world already. They tell us we can be criticized for taking a stand. I tell you that we join this day with Christians across the land to light a candle in the cause of peace, in the hope that the One who lit Bethlehem's fields with a holy light may make his brilliant presence felt among us in a troubled time once more.

(Congregation stands. Music continues while ushers light the candles of the first persons in each pew. The light is passed until all candles are lighted. All sing "Joy to the World" and leave with lighted candles.)

A Christmas eve celebration. Suggested worship center is a life-size cradle and a plain bench with one 7-candle candelabra behind and to the left a bit. Choir sits in section of congregation. Candles are given to persons as they enter. Narrators speak in loud clear voices from seats in congregation.

the most treasured Gift

(lights dim as candles are lighted and congregation begins to sing JOY TO THE WORLD, vs. 1.)

Voice 1:   The Lord is in his holy temple; let all the earth be silent before him. Glory to God in the highest heaven, they said, and peace on earth for all those pleasing him.

Song: "Let All Mortal Flesh Keep Silence," stanzas 1 and 2, by the congregation.

Voice 2:   The people who walk in darkness shall see a great light--a light that will shine on all those who live in the land of the shadow of death. The royal line of David will be cut off, chopped down like a tree, but from the stump will grow a shoot, yes, a new branch from the old root. And the Spirit of the Lord shall rest upon him--the Spirit of wisdom, understanding, counsel and might, the spirit of knowledge and of the fear of the Lord.

Song: "Lo, How a Rose E'er Blooming," by the choir

Voice 1:   And because Joseph was a member of the royal line, he had to go to Bethlehem in Judea, King David's ancient home, journeying there from the Galilean village of Nazareth. He took with him Mary, his fiancee, who was obviously pregnant by this time. She gave birth to her first child. She wrapped him in a blanket and laid him in a manger because there was no room for them in the village inn.

(A man and woman with a small baby enter and place the baby in the cradle)

Song: "O Little Town of Bethlehem," by the congregation

Voice 3:   God must really have trusted this young couple from Nazareth, to place his most treasured gift in their keeping. For they were poor and they had to travel to Bethlehem in Judea without any hotel reservations to insure a comfortable place for Mary. There was danger all the way--from highwaymen and robbers; from the hardships of travel; from the thoughtlessness of soldiers; from a king who was quickly aroused to murderous decrees.

Song: "Silent Night, Holy Night," sung by the father to his wife and child

Voice 2:   And yet God entrusted this gift for the world to a young man and woman who had little to recommend them except their love for each other and the child that should be born. They could summon no servants to run for a physician, they had no letters of introduction to hotel managers, they had no money to spare for bribes. Consequently, they were turned away from the inn and forced to find lodging in a barn. God left his treasure with two young people who had no privileges whatsoever.

Voice 1:   In the stillness of a night that God made bright with a star, Mary gave birth to the child, unattended except by Joseph and the sleepy cattle across the room. But Mary was a mother and Joseph was a husband; and every mother knows her child is a gift from God, a treasure for the world. So God had been wise after all. Of course, there was danger abroad, but there was only love in Mary's heart. And the gift of God was wrapped in the love that every parent knows.

Song: "Mary, Rock-a-Your Baby," by the choir

Voice 3:   So rich has been the treasure of this child that now we look back at that first Christmas and see only beauty and light, for we have heard the angel song and seen the kneeling Magi from the East. But let us not forget that Mary suffered that night, and Joseph paced the stable floor, and there were moments of dark indecision before the light came.

Voice 1:   That night some shepherds were in the fields outside the village, guarding their flocks of sheep. Suddenly an angel appeared among them, and the landscape shone bright with the glory of the Lord. They were badly frightened, but the angel reassured them. "Don't be afraid! I bring you the most joyful news ever announced, and it is for everyone! The Savior-yes, the Messiah, the Lord-has been born tonight in Bethlehem!"

Song: "Angels We Have Heard on High," flute duet
(Little children come and stand around the cradle while the flutes are playing)

Song: "Away in a Manger," by children around the cradle

Voice 1:   The shepherds said "Come on, let's go to Bethlehem. Let's see this wonderful thing that has happened. They ran to the village and found their way to Mary and Joseph, and there was the baby, lying in a manger.

Voice 2:   If God would share his richest gift with a mother and father of Nazareth, will he not also honor our hearts and our homes with his presence? We have only to open our doors and the everlasting light will shine in.

Song: "I Heard the Bells on Christmas Day," by a soloist

(During the singing, four choir members go to the lighted candelabra and light their candles. They then go out into the congregation, lighting the candle of the person at the end of each row so that light will be shared all across the row. When candles are all lighted, the congregation stands for the benediction.)

Voice 3:   Lord, let the warmth and the beauty of Christmas penetrate our lives;
let something of what the shepherds experienced on that Judean hillside long
ago be a "happening" for us in these moments; let the anticipation of Mary and
the glad rejoicing of the wise men come to fulfillment in our midst; let the
renewal of hope that comes to Israel and the "good news of a great joy which will
come to all the people" come now to fulfillment in us. Amen. Amen.

Song (for recessional): *"Joy to the World"*

*(The reading parts are taken from Habakkuk, Isaiah, and Luke from the Bible, and
from the story, "Most Treasured Gift," by Kenneth I. Morse, Messenger, December 1974)*

Variations and Ideas
for candlelighting services

*Begin the candlelighting service in darkness with a voice reading Genesis 1:1-5,
followed by the congregation singing the Doxology in unison. Then begin a
procession of candle bearers a few at a time as the worship progresses until the
entire church is lighted. Complete with a carol of joy.*

Have each family bring its own candle to church on Christmas eve. Upon entering
the sanctuary, light the candle from a large white Christ candle, then proceed
to place it in holders provided. These candles provide the only light for the
service. At the close, a member of each family may take his "light" and process
from the sanctuary with his or her family, leaving the sanctuary in darkness
except for the Christ candle.

Search for a Christmas King

by Andy Murray

Flutes: ("We Three Kings," stanza 1 [unison], stanza 2 and chorus, background till narrator is finished.)

Narrator: In the latter days of 1970 there were three young astrologers who deduced from their study of books and stars that a king would be found somewhere in the great Pacific Northwest. So they journeyed from their home in Memphis, Tenn. to Portland in the land of Oregon, bearing gifts--a box of Indian incense, a Bob Dylan record, and a copy of *The Prophet*. Having no idea where to look first, or really what they were looking for, they went to the Chamber of Commerce to inquire after their king.

The Chamber of Commerce was perplexed about the strange request of the young men but the quick-thinking attractive young lady behind the desk answered politely:

Young Girl: Surely you will find what you are looking for in one of our great department stores. For they have unlimited resources to fulfill the fondest dram of every man. You can find there a fondue set or a belt with a peace symbol buckle. You can find a book on love, assorted candy, and fashion boots. Surely they will have your king. And go and search diligently for it; and when you have found it, return and tell us, for it sounds like there may be some real potential here for a new promotional campaign for our city.

Flutes: (Finish at end of narration)

Band: ("We Three Kings" one stanza)

Drums:

Guitar: (for eight measures during showing of slides: plane landing, wise men leaving air port, hitchhiking, downtown, department sotre, Santa Claus)

Band: ("We Three Kings", two stanzas)

Band and singers: ("We Three Kings," stanza 1 and chorus, stanza 2 and chorus)

SCENE ONE: "The Department Store"

(A setting may be created using a shelf with a toy machine gun, a stuffed dove, and a boxed game.)

Santa: Ho, ho, ho! Merry Christmas. And what would you like for Chirstmas, little fellow?

Little boy: Gee, Santa, I want a fire truck and a puppy dog.

Santa: Have you been a good little boy this year?

Little boy: Oh yes, Santa.

Santa: I'm sure you were a good little boy. I'll leave these at your house for Christmas. And what's your name, little girl?

Little girl: Shirley.

Santa: And what do you want for Chirstmas, Shirley?

Little girl: I wanna baby-laugh-a-boo dollie and a rocking horsey.

Santa: If you've been a good little girl this year, Santa will see what he can do. Bye.

First wise man: Excuse me, sir. We're looking for a king, and we were told we might find him here. Can you help us?

Second wise man: You're dressed in an odd way. Are you perhaps the king?

Santa: I guess you could call me that. I make kids happy. I tell them what they want to hear.

Third wise man: You actually buy all those presents for those kids?

Santa: Are you crazy? Their parents buy their gifts for them. I just pretend I'm giving them the presents. Don't you know what Christmas is all about?

First wise man: Could you tell us? Perhaps it would help us find our king.

Santa: Look around you. Listen to the carols on the intercom. Look at the happy shoppers. (Long pause) Now, must you ask what Christmas is about?

Second wise man: What do these kids get from these toys?

Santa: Pleasure, enjoyment, fun, satisfaction....

Third wise man: (interrupting) But that's what our king is supposed to give. Are you sure they get that from toys?

Santa: Sure, kids are happy when they have a lot of toys.

First wise man: But our king is supposed to give us power.

Santa: First floor toy department. Johnny Super Sub Sonic Machine Gun. Enough power to make any kid a king. (1st wise man picks up gun)

Second wise man: But our king is supposed to give us peace.

Santa: (beginning to get impatient) Second floor notions. Get a stuffed dove.

Third wise man: But our king is supposed . . .

Santa: (interrupting) Listen, I know what you fellows need. Third floor adult games. Get that new game "King for a Day". That'll fix you.

Band and singers: *("We Three Kings , R.S.V.")*

    Old Saint Nick has done it again,
    Warning the kids that they'd better make friends.
    Be nice and be good as you know you should,
    Or you won't get your presents at all.

    Oh, Star of guns and dolls and trains,
    Star of spoiled children's games,
    Where is it leading? Greed is increasing,
    Guide us to the department store lights.

Narrator: The three astrologers then inquired of a nearby standing cabdriver if
    he knew where they might find the Christmas king. The cabby answered with a
    knowing wink and a smile. "Sure fellows, hop right in, take you right to him.
    Its best if you bring along a little something though. Know what I mean?"
    The astrologers replied that they had gifts and so the driver took them to
    a fashionable home in the suburbs.

Band: *("We Three Kings," one stanza Nashville Sound during showing of slides:*
    Getting in taxi, city streets & lights, going up to home)

SCENE TWO: *"At the Party"*

(Wise man knocks on door. Picture changes, and man is in doorway. On the shelf
now is a liquor bottle, a record album, and a party hat.)

Man: Yeah, what can I do for you?

Second wise man: Excuse me, this may seem odd to you, but we're looking for
    a king.

Man: Far out. You fellows are ready for a big one, huh?

Second wise man: I beg your pardon.

Man: King of the bash - that's me, man. You're in the right place. The party
    price. This is where it's happening. Say, uh, you brought a little something
    didn't you?

Third wise man: Yes, some gifts. We brought a Bob Dylan record, a box of incense,
    and a copy of *The Prophet.*

Man: Well, that isn't going to get you fellows much of a party now.

Third wise man: But we're not looking for a party. We're looking for the king.

Man: Oh, we got that. Right there. Help yourself. (Wise man picks up record
    album) B.B. King. (sings) "the thrill is gone." We got the King family,
    Alan King, The Kingsmen.

First wise man: I'm afraid we're looking for a king of a little different sort.
    One who brings peace and joy and satisfaction for the spirit.

Man: Right. Right. Right over there. (Wise man picks up bottle) Guaranteed
    to bring you peace, joy, and all the satisfactory Christmas spirit you can
    handle. That's the best stuff. Top of the line. Cheer you when you're
    lonely and warm you when you're cold. Well, what do you say? **107**

Second wise man: I'm afraid we're at the wrong place.

Man: You fellows are sure hard to please, aren't you? (Wise men walk slowly away)
Go find your peace and joy but it won't be much of a party, I'll guarantee you
that. Ha, ha. Bunch of hippie subversives.

Drums:
Band and singers: *("We Three Kings RSV")*

> At the office at home or the bar
> Christmas parties have gone too far,
> Drinking, joking, profanely praising the
> Spirit of Christmas day
> > Oh, Star of egg nog mixed with beer,
> > Star of bourbon balls spiked with good cheer,
> > Westbound speeding and increasing
> > Guide us to the night club lights.

Narrator: Discouraged and thinking they had perhaps miscalculated, the three
astrologers discussed among themselves whether they should try one more place.
They heard singing from a nearby church and decided to ask there if anyone knew
where a king might be found.

Band with flutes: *("We Three Kings" one stanza during showing slides: wise men
walking street, church, wise men approaching church, inside of church, minister
in pulpit)*

SCENE THREE: "In the Church"

Minister: And now before we close this Christmas service I would like to give
some announcements. First of all, I would like to thank the youth group for
providing the tree and other greenery which decorates the church. I also want
to thank the Johnson family for their very generous gift of providing the
catering services for this evening's coffee hour. Mr. & Mrs. Johnson, by the
way, are spending the Christmas vacation in Hawaii celebrating their tenth
anniversary. I'm sure they will appreciate your prayers for a safe and happy
journey. I hope you will all plan to come to the "Giving Supper" next Thursday.
We are working toward a new Sunday school wing. If you would like to help,
please contact Mrs. Janet Wells or Mrs. Joyce Stemm. Now if there is nothing
more shall we . . .

Third wise man: Excuse me! We are strangers to your city, and we have spent the
day searching for the Christmas King.

First wise man: The Chamber of Commerce hasn't been able to help us, and we have
discovered nothing in your social gatherings. We were told we could find what
we're looking for here. It must be a precious secret. Could you share it with us?

Minister: You're looking for the Christmas King? Well, it's right there.

Second wise man: (Going over very slowly and taking the doll from the manger.
Camera close up on the doll) This is just a doll. It, it's not even real.
What kind of a joke is this?

Third wise man: We've come all the way from Memphis looking for a king who could
bring peace, joy, and love to the world, and you have the nerve to show us a
doll baby.

First wise man: Keep your doll. (He takes it and goes over to place it in the
    manger)

Band and singers: ("We Three Kings" RSV)

    We've searched the town for the real Christmas King
    Asked the people but they know nothing
    Went to God's house but his spirit was out
    For an evening walk in the dark.
        Oh Star of churches that cease to proclaim,
        Star of dwindling candle flame,
        In search of a manger, outcast by strangers,
        Guide us to thy chapel lights.

                EPILOGUE: *"The King is Found"*

*(The scene is the same as Scene Three. The wise men are walking away from the
minister.)*

Band and singers: *"Your Brother's the One"* (Music available on the record
    "Summertime Children" by Andy Murray, Brethren Press. Words used by permission.)

    Chorus:

    Reach out and touch somebody's hand.
    Look into somebody's eyes.
    The King is walking through the land
    And it should come as no surprise. . .
        That he's working with your brother's hands
        And he's seeing with your brother's eyes.
    If you're waiting for the king to come. . .
                    Your brother's the one.

    You can look up, and you can look down
    You can go all over, this old town.
                    But you'll never find
                    The Christmas King
                    Till you've a mind
                    To do one thing.

    Chorus

    You can see lights, you can see trees,
    Artificial snow, up to your knees,
                    But you'll never see
                    The manger child
                    Till all brothers are free
                    And reconciled.

    Chorus

    You can buy presents, you can buy toys,
    Guns, dolls, and trains, for the girls and boys.
                    But they won't have a thing
                    They can enjoy
                    Till they see the king
                    In every girl and boy.

    Chorus

Arman and the Three Wisemen

a play for puppets by
Galene J. Myers

Scene: The Well of the Magi outside Bethlemen

Time: After the birth of Jesus

Characters: Arman, a young shepherd lad, lame in his right foot
  Mara, his mother
  Caspar, Melchior, Balthazar, the three Wise Men

Scenery: The town of Bethlehem. A well of papier-mache is in the fore-
  ground.

Music: The carols suggested in the play may be "sung by the puppets" sung
  by children behind the scenes, or played from a recording.

Scene 1

(Mara *is seated on the rim of the well. Carol: "Christ was born on Christmas
  day" [14th century German carol]. After the song there is a moment of silence, then sounds of camel bells and voices.)*

Mara: Arman, Arman, come quickly! I hear camel bells and voices approaching.

Arman: Coming, mother. There is a magnificent caravan resting yonder below
  the path. There are three kings wearing long capes-a tall old man, a
  young man, and a black man. Come here, mother. Look beyond the brush!

Mara: Yes, yes, I see them! They seem to be searching the sky. Perhaps for
  that new star we have seen. Go quickly. Bring them to the well.

Arman: I'll offer them a drink of cool water.

Mara: *(leaning over the well)*: Tell them that the star is reflected in the water
  of the well.

(Arman *exits and soon there is a sound of bells and the music of "We three kings.")*

Arman*(returning)*: Mother, these three kings wish to speak to you.

(The Wisemen *enter to the singing of "We Three Kings," stanza 1 and refrain.)*

Caspar: I am Caspar from the far East.

Melchior: I am Melchior of the near East.

Balthazar: I am Balthazar of Ethiopia.

Mara: Welcome, Wise Men, welcome.

Arman: The star, the star! See, it is reflected in the well.

Melchior: We have followed the star a long way. We seek a newborn king. We
    come to worship him.

(Carol: Stanzas 2,3, and 4 of "We three kings." It concludes with the refrain.)

Caspar: We inquired of King Herod in Jerusalem. His advisers quoted an old
    prophecy about Bethlehem. Do you know about that?

Mara: Yes, yes, I know the prophecy. The prophet Micah said, "But you, O
    Bethlehem Ephrathah, who are little to be among the clans of Judah, from
    you shall come forth for me one who is to be ruler in Israel."

Balthazar: Have you seen or heard of such a ruler, a newborn king?

Mara: Could it possibly be the child born that holy night when angels sang?

Balthazar: Herod asked us to report back to him, so that he could worship
    this king also.

Arman: Do not trust King Herod for he murdered...

Mara: Hush, Arman, hush. One cannot speak against the king and live.

Melchior: Have no fear, young man. We have been warned in a dream that Herod
    seeks the young child's life. We shall return via Hebron and travel south
    of the Red Sea.

Caspar: Tell us more about the angel tidings, the night when the king was born.

Arman: I heard the angels that night while keeping our sheep. I took the
    first watch, for my father is old and our sheep are many. At midnight I
    was studying the stars for I shall be an astrologer some day. Suddenly a
    brilliant light appeared. In its radiance angels sang and spoke, "Be not
    afraid; for to you is born this day in the city of David a Savior, who is
    Christ the Lord. You will find a babe wrapped in swaddling cloths and lying
    in a manger."

(Carol: "Shepherds shake off your drowsy sleep" {old French carol})

Melchior: What glory that must have been! Did you go to Bethlehem to see
    the child?

Arman: Yes, I ran with the others, but my lame leg made me slow. I saw the
    babe in all his splendor with Mary and Joseph.

Mara: I have seen him, too. This child is our Messiah without a doubt.

Arman: Look, the star hangs above the house where the child stays.

Balthazar: Thank you, thank you, Arman. No king would look for a royal
    price in a humble house. Would you guide us to this lowly place?

Arman: Mother, may I go? May I guide them to the Christ child? Then I'll
    go to the hills immediately.

Mara: Very well, Arman, but your father needs you when he sleeps.

Melchior: We'll remember. Come, Arman, it is growing late. We'll return in the early morning before we start the caravan.

(The Wise Men and Arman leave. Mara watches from the well. Carol: "O Little town of Bethlehem.")

Scene 2

(Mara is at the well. Carol: "Lully, lulla, thou little tiny child," [the Coventry Carol]. Arman enters.)

Mara: You are early, my son.

Arman: I know. I wish to see the caravan leave.

(The Wise Men enter. Background music: "We three kings.")

Caspar: Thank you!

Melchior: Thank you!

Balthazar: Thank you!

Caspar: We have seen the newborn king. We have worshiped him.

Melchior: Arman, we wish to give you a gift because you led us to the child. Here is money to pay the scribe in Bethlehem to teach you reading, writing, and the study of the stars.

Caspar: Here is a ring with a royal seal to mark the letters you will send to us. On this tablet are the directions to use.

Balthazar: Here are the tools for writing you will need-some papyrus, a reed pen, an ink palette, a sponge, and a knife. With care these will last for years. We wish you well in your studies.

Arman: Thank you Caspar, Melchior, and Balthazar.

Mara: From my heart I thank you three kings. Now my son will be a scholar, a scribe, and one who studies the stars. His lame leg will hinder him no longer.

Balthazar: Yes, he will overcome his handicap with great success.

The Wise Men begin to leave. Carol begins: "March of the Kings" [old French carol]. Arman waves goodbye.)

Arman: Farewell, kind kings, farewell.
   (Carol: "March of the Kings.")

_____

The above puppet play is reprinted from *Christmas Is Coming*, compiled by Katherine J. Waller, copyright 1971 by Augsburg Publishing House, Minneapolis, Minnesota. Used by permission.

International Celebrations

and Traditions

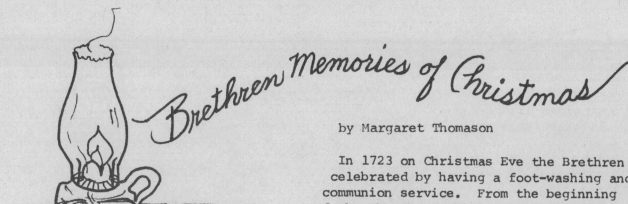

Brethren Memories of Christmas

by Margaret Thomason

In 1723 on Christmas Eve the Brethren celebrated by having a foot-washing and communion service. From the beginning of the Church of the Brethren through most of the 19th Century, Christmas for Brethren was a somber occasion. It was much like a typical Sunday--attending church both in the morning and evening. There were no exchanges of gifts, no special food, no gaiety.

In E.E. Emmert's diaries, each year he wrote-in: "CHRISTMAS." He wrote who the speaker was at church for the morning and evening services and what scripture was read. Some years he wrote about having dinner with certain neighbors. Some Christmases he wrote that there was a baptismal service; other Christmases he mentioned performing marriages. In 1891 he received a silver watch on Christmas day -- the only time he mentioned a gift.

Edith Barnes said she read in her mother's diary recently that she got an orange and candy on her plate on Christmas morning. In 1880 she wrote about exchanging gifts. It was a simple, homemade gift that was given.

Edith remembers their first Christmas tree. In 1900 her aunt from Philadelphia came to their home and put up a tree and decorated it after the children had gone to bed. As early as 1903 she recalls their parents gave them something small on Christmas.

Clyde Weaver said he doesn't remember anything special about Christmas in their home. He said it was always a time of being with family and relatives. (But this wasn't only typical of Brethren). It was always time of eating lots of food -- Pennsylvania Dutch seven sweets and seven sours. There was much over-indulging in eating -- "their only way to sin." It was one harmful thing they could do that was okay. Still along the eating line he recalls there were always loads and loads of cookies that were made and shared around. He doesn't remember any special kind of cookies that were Christmas specialties. (Again, he said this wasn't just Brethren who made cookies, but everyone did.) He remembers, too, that he got an orange and candy but this was not at home or church. These were given out at a community affair at the firehouse.

In talking with Stewart Kauffman about what he remembers about Christmas, he said he grew up believing in Santa Claus. Not until he was an older child, did he know what Christmas was all about.

I was unable to find out how and when the Brethren changed from the serious, religious observance of Christmas to the celebration of today. Apparently there has been a very gradual change, with Brethren in some areas including "worldly" ways and festivities years sooner than other areas.

Christmas Treats

by Margaret Thomason

DATE PINWHEELS

½ c. butter
½ c. brown sugar
½ c. granulated sugar
1 egg
½ tsp. vanilla
2 c. sifted flour
½ tsp. soda
½ tsp. salt
1 recipe of date filling

Thoroughly cream butter and sugars.
Add egg and vanilla; beat well. Sift
dry ingredients together and stir into creamed mixture. Chill. Divide
dough in half. On lightly floured
surface, roll one part in 8x12" rectangle, about ¼" thick. Spread half
of date filling over dough. Begin at
long edge, roll like jelly roll. Repeat with remaining dough and filling.
Wrap rolls in waxed paper. Chill several hours. Slice ¼" thick. Bake
on greased cookie sheet at 400° a-
bout 8 minutes. Makes 5 doz.

APRICOT DELIGHTS

1 lb. dried apricots
1 lb. sugar
1 orange

Grind apricots and orange. Add sugar. Let stand a short time. Add
2 or 3 tbsp. water. Cook slowly
for 10 min. Put 1 tsp. of mixture
into sugar or coconut and coat.
Shape into balls.

PARISIAN SWEETS

1 pkg. dates (10 oz.)
¼ lb. shredded coconut
½ c. chopped nuts
½ lb. figs
1 tbsp. orange juice
1 tbsp. grated orange rind

Chop dates, figs and coconut. Knead
together with orange juice and rind.
Shape into 1-inch balls and roll in
shredded coconut.

FRIED APPLE PIES

2 c. dried apples
2/3 c. sugar
1 tsp. cinnamon
½ tsp. cloves
regular pastry

Soak apples in 1½ c. warm water several hours. Add sugar, cinnamon and
cloves. Cook until done and not too
watery. Cool. Make regular pastry.
Roll out a ball about the size of a
large hen egg. Use a saucer to cut
dough into circular shape. Add 2
or 3 tbsp. apples to one half the
dough circle. Turn other half over
to form half moon tart shape. Seal
edge. Press around the edge with
ends of fork tines. Make 3 pricks
with fork in top of pie to allow air
to escape. Fry in skillet in moderately hot fat. Brown on both sides.
Cool and eat.

115

Sand tarts

½ c. butter
1 c. sugar
1 egg
1 tbsp. cream
½ tsp. vanilla
Mix together ½ tsp. salt
    1 tsp. baking powder
    1½ c. flour

Beat butter, sugar, egg, cream, and vanilla until creamy. Add the dry ingredients and mix well. (Slightly soft.) Roll into a roll 1½" in diameter. Chill.

Slice 1/8" thick. Place on cookie sheet. Brush with beaten egg and place an almond half on top or sprinkle with mixture of 1tbsp. sugar, ¼ tsp. cinnamon. (Cookies may be rolled out thin and cut with cookie cutters.)
Bake at 375° for 5 - 8 minutes. Approximately 60 cookies.

by Helen Kauffman

Rocks

1 c. butter
1 c. lt. brown sugar
3 eggs, well beaten
1 tsp. vanilla
½ tsp. salt
2¼ c. flour
½ tsp. soda
1 tsp. cinnamon
1 c. chopped raisins
1 c. chopped walnuts.

Cream butter and sugar. Add eggs, vanilla and salt. Add the combined flour, soda and cinnamon. Add raisins and nuts.
Drop by spoon onto greased cookie sheet. Bake at 350° about 10 minutes. (Store in tightly closed can with an apple.) Approximately 60 cookies.

Though Brethren historically have not given a lot of gifts at Christmas, they were very fine craftsmen and each practical thing that was created for the home and family was made well. We have created patterns for a brother and sister doll, complete with plain dress and enclose a plan for a "Dutch" cradle that can be made for a life size baby or made small of cardboard for little Christmas favors.

Brother and Sister dolls

For 14" dolls, 1 sq. = 1"
For 20" dolls, 1 sq. = 1½"
¼" seam allowances on all patterns.
Suggested fabrics: For body, pink
cotton or cotton blend, velveteen or
flannel. Stuff with polyester fiber, cotton batting, or old nylon
stockings.

Clothing: cotton or blends of plain
colored material. Possibly double
knit scraps for brother's coat and
trousers. Felt for suspenders, shoes
and brother's hat. Sister's bonnet
and apron should be white.
Satin stitch in eyes, mouth and
nose. Use yarn for hair, stitched
so it looks like it is parted in
the middles. Sister's hair
should have a bun in the back
and brother's hang to shoulder.
You can add a beard if you wish.

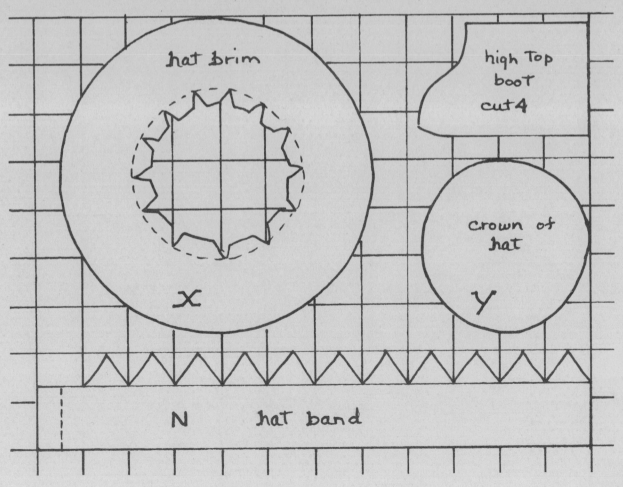

hat brim

high Top
boot
cut 4

crown of
hat

X

Y

N   hat band

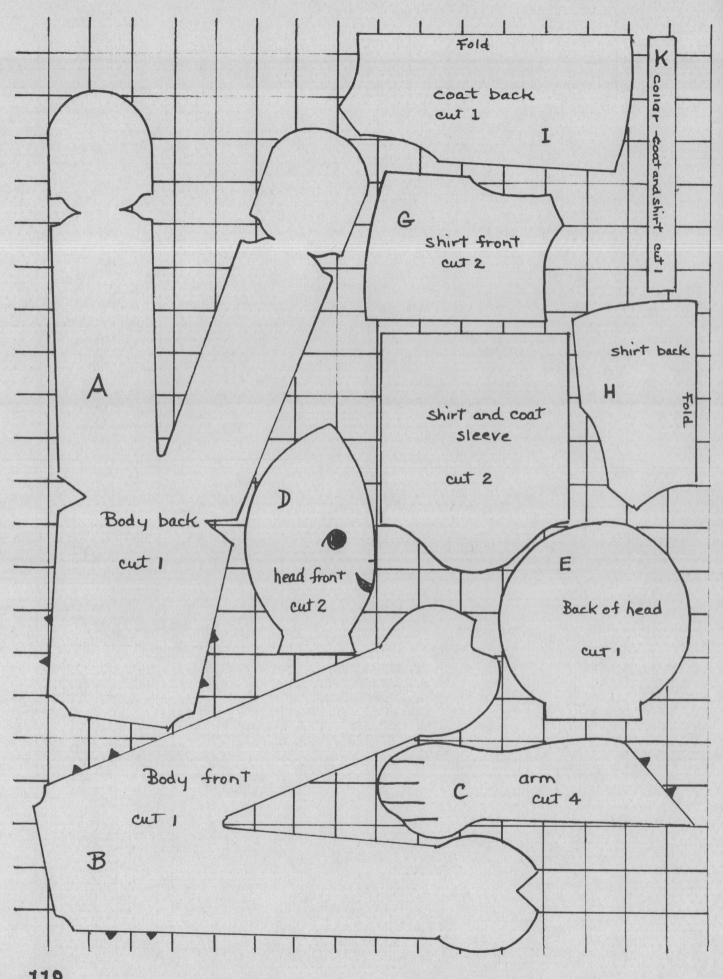

Fold

coat back
cut 1

I

K
collar coat and shirt cut 1

G
shirt front
cut 2

shirt back

H

Fold

A

Body back

cut 1

D

head front

cut 2

Shirt and coat
sleeve

cut 2

E

Back of head

cut 1

Body front

cut 1

B

C

arm
cut 4

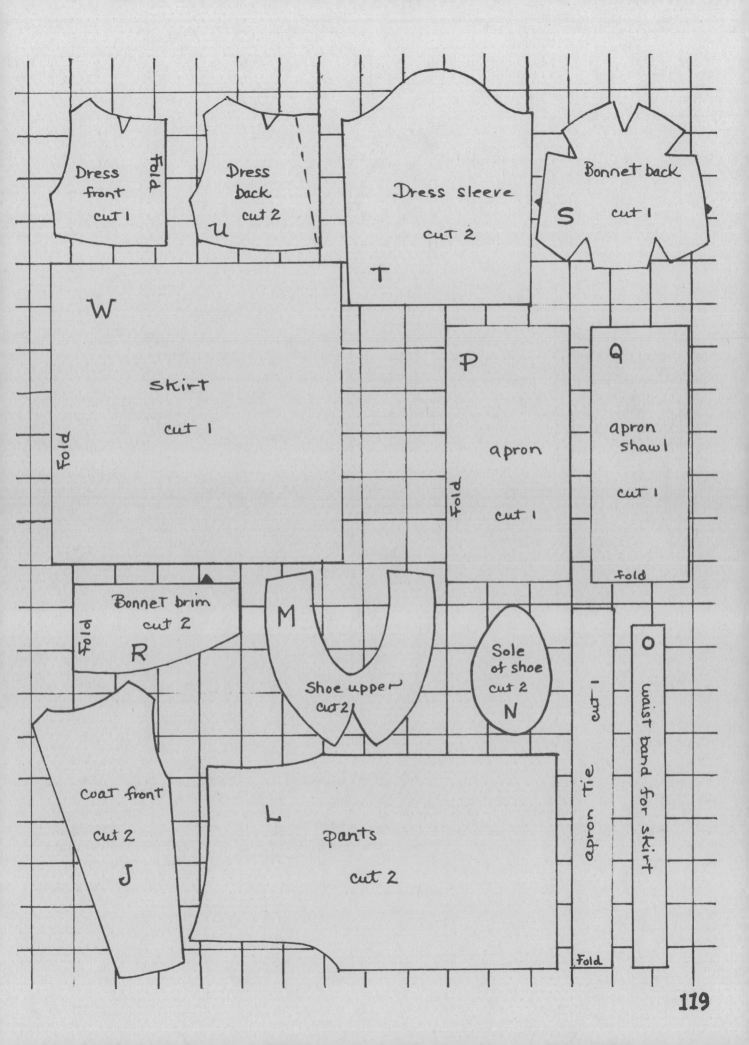

Dress front cut 1

Dress back cut 2 — Fold — U

Dress sleeve cut 2 — T

Bonnet back cut 1 — S

W — Skirt cut 1 — Fold

P — apron cut 1 — Fold

Q — apron shawl cut 1 — fold

Bonnet brim cut 2 — Fold — R

M — Shoe upper cut 2

Sole of shoe cut 2 — N

O — waist band for skirt

apron tie cut 1 — Fold

Coat front cut 2 — J

L — pants cut 2

To make doll body, sew darts
on body back (A)

Sew front of head together (D),
turn and sew to body front (B).
Sew head back to body back.

Sew arm pieces together (C) turn,
stuff and quilt in fingers with
machine. Pin arms to body back
on right side matching notches.
Face body front right side down on top of arms and back and stitch all around
except 2½" length under one arm.
This is left to turn doll right side
out and as stuffing hole. Turn and
stuff firmly and over cast under arm
seam to close opening.

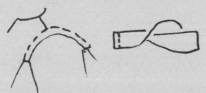

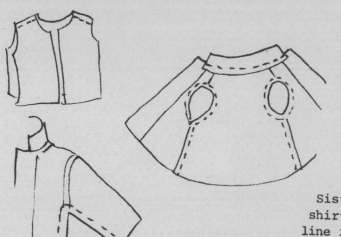

Shirt: Attach shoulder seams, set
in sleeves. Sew arm and side seams.
Turn under shirt fron ¼" to made
facing. Snaps may be sewn on as
fasteners. Fold collar in half,
stitch ends, turn and sew to shirt
neckline. Hem shirt ¼".
Make coat in same way.

Sister's dress top is assembled same as
shirt except opening is in back and neckline is just stitched under (no collar);
gather skirt and sew to top. Sew up seam 2/3
way from hem to top of dress. Turn under rest
of open seams to make facing and use snaps as
fasteners.

120

Bonnet: Sew in darts on (S)
Sew brim together, turn and match notches with
(S); sew brim to bonnet back, turn and stitch
hem in bottom.

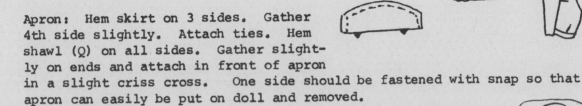

Apron: Hem skirt on 3 sides. Gather
4th side slightly. Attach ties. Hem
shawl (Q) on all sides. Gather slightly on ends and attach in front of apron
in a slight criss cross.   One side should be fastened with snap so that
apron can easily be put on doll and removed.

Pants: Put right sides together. Sew,
then fold and sew leg seams. Hem top
and bottom.

Make suspenders from felt or leather
to look like diagram. Fasten inside
trousers front and back.

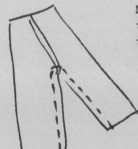

Brother's hat: Cut out of heavy black paper
and felt. Trim flaps off felt and glue to
paper. Score paper on dotted lines (brim).
Fold flaps up. Glue band to it. Fold in
flaps on band and glue on crown.

Shoes: (M,N) Stitch in dart and back. Sew to
sole, clip seams and turn. Hightop boot goes
together much the same way.

121

"Dutch" Cradle

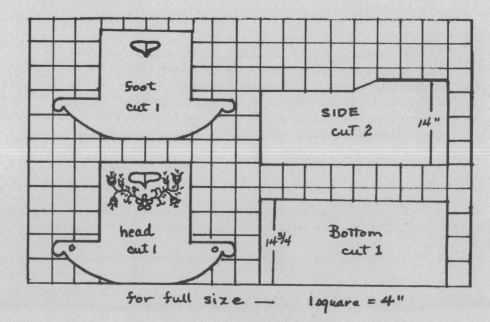

foot
cut 1

SIDE
cut 2

14"

head
cut 1

14 3/4

Bottom
cut 1

for full size — 1 square = 4"

For full size cradle, you will need a 4' x 6' piece of 5/8" plywood, 2-1" diameter dowels, 33¼" long. The dimensions are as above and should be nailed and glued together as diagram. All edges may be finished with wood tape. Apply according to instructions. Cradle may be stained any desired color, varnished and designs painted on with model enamels or acrylic paints.

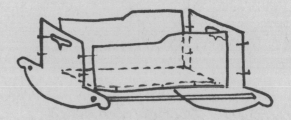

Cradle can also be made doll size. Use grid pattern and use as key, 1 square=2". Make from ¼" plywood.

Or, you can make table decorations that hold candy or crackers for gifts by using key of 1 square = 1". Make these from heavy cardboard or 1/8" paneling scraps. Tape and glue joints and paint with acrylic paints.

122

Christmas with the Navajo

The Navajo are in the process of creating a tradition for Christmas. They have no unique way of their own, no similar feast day with which to adapt as have other traditions.

The Navajo come from centuries of belief in the totality of nature. They believe in a type of eternal life in which the spirit takes on a new form after death. As missionaries have brought the news of Christ, a new tradition has begun to be established, basically from the traditions of the missionaries themselves.

Children have learned of Christmas at school and church. Their Christmas programs and parties are similar to those all over the United States. Gift giving which is also not an original Navajo custom has been adopted from the Christians in a simple way, including yard goods for making clothes, candy, nuts, fruits, and toys.

The Navajo are fine craftsmen. They make jewelry, pottery and beautiful woven rugs, purses, blankets, and baskets from yarn or grasses. They make their own garments and are very skillful with beadwork and design. But many of the things they make are for personal use or to be sold to make a living.

Christmas day is a family kind of celebration, again similar to all the peoples of this country, with one exception. The special native feast foods of mutton stew and Navajo fried bread are served along with many familiar American Christmas foods.

Included here are recipes for mutton stew and Navajo fried bread. Also a pattern for a Navajo doll complete with costume.

Navajo Fried Bread

1 tsp. salt
2 c. flour
2 tsp. baking powder

Mix together and put a hole in the middle, add about 1 c. water, or enough to be able to knead into a ball. Pat into thin circular patties. Fry in about ½" hot fat melted in the bottom of a heavy frying pan. Fry till bubbles and turn and fry till lightly browned. Drain on paper towel Serve hot with stew. Delicious with butter and jam.

Mutton Stew

Cut 3 lb. of lamb in 1" cubes, season with salt and pepper. Cover with boiling water and simmer for ½ hour. Add 1 c. each carrots, onions, potatoes, peas or any mix of vegetables should be cut in thick slices or cubes. Simmer 30 minutes until the vegetables are done.

The Navajo also like to serve hot peppers with their stew.

NAVAJO DOLL is made from the same pattern as the "brother" and "sister" dolls,
except using light brown material for the
body. The dress top is made from velveteen and the skirt from calico or taf-
feta. The skirt is gathered with a
band and a back opening. Fasten with
a hook or snap. Top is worn over
skirt, has a front opening. Little
strands of turquoise beads may be
made of baker's clay and strung on
dental floss. Moccasins may be made
of felt or velveteen.

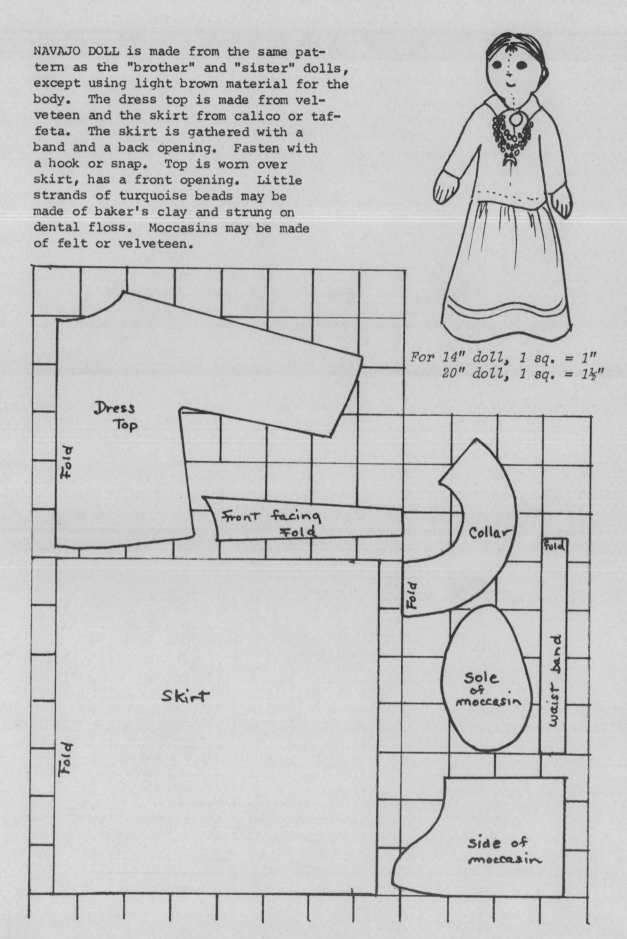

For 14" doll, 1 sq. = 1"
20" doll, 1 sq. = 1½"

Dress Top

Fold

Front facing Fold

Collar

Fold

Skirt

Fold

Fold

waist band

Sole of moccasin

side of moccasin

Germany

By Dora Klostermeyer

The German celebration of Christmas begins with the first Sunday of Advent. The family gathers together to make the traditional wreath of spruce branches. This wreath hangs by four red ribbons from the ceiling or on a special little stand, constructed to sit on the table. Sometimes the wreath is placed on a large plate, and the center is filled with fruit and nuts. The wreath always has four red candles and may also be decorated with four red bows. Starting with the first Sunday, one candle is lighted, lighting one more the next Sunday and so on.

On the 6th of December, St. Nicholas Day is celebrated. St. Nicholas was known for secretly leaving gifts for poor children at Christmas time. On that evening, German children put their shoes outside on the doorstep or on the wide window ledge. During the night St. Nicholas visits, leaving nuts and candies in the shoes.

On Christmas eve all families go to church services. Songs are sung and pageants of the Nativity are presented. When the families come home from services, the Christmas tree is lighted. They still use small wax candles on their Christmas trees, so the length of time that they are lighted is very short. The Christmas tree is always spruce, no pines are used. The trees are decorated with hand-made ornaments in the shapes of stars, angels, little Santas, etc. They are made from silver and gold papers. Many of the decorations are cookies and little candies called "sugar kringles". Sometimes decorations are also made of straw or gilded nuts.

After lighting the tree, Santa appears, often with the Christ child played by a small child dressed like an angel all in white and a halo on its head. The children are afraid of Santa because he carries a stick along with his large bag. If a child doesn't behave, Santa threatens him or her with the stick. The children all learn little verses to recite to Santa as a welcome. Very often the verses contain statements to the effect that they will be very good and pay attention to their parents. Then Santa puts his stick away and opens his sack to hand out presents to the children. Presents are never wrapped. The children thank Santa and offer him cookies and milk before he leaves. Then the children give gifts to their parents that have been secretly made. Many times these little gifts take weeks to make in some hidden place where no one could find out what the precious gift would be. Fathers would receive hand made sweaters, socks and gloves from their daughters. The girls would make shawls, gloves, sweaters, doilies that were either crocheted or knit. The boys would make shelves, picture frames, little boxes key racks, even lamps for the table. The smaller children made potholders, pen holders, bookends and little notebooks. After the gift exchange, supper is served. It is usually a light meal, but always contains something very special that has been saved just for Christmas eve.

Christmas morning the family again goes to church. At noon time a special dinner is served, often with a roasted stuffed goose as the main course. Children are always presented with tiny little marzipan piglets as a gift on Chirstmas day. Every family enjoys the traditional Christmas Stollen, a sweetbread made of yeast dough with raisins, almonds and candied citron fruit. Also Lebkuchen and the marzipan candies.

Included is a recipe for German Stollen, Nürnberger Lebkuchen and the mar- zipan candies. There are directions for making the hanging Advent wreath, a wooden key rack and a little chicken potholder that roosts right on a pan handle.

Stollen

(heat oven to 375°)
1 pkg. dry yeast
3/4 c. warm water
½ c. sugar
½ tsp. salt
3 eggs
1 egg yolk (reserve white)
½ c. soft butter
3½ c. flour
½ c. blanched chopped almonds
¼ c. cut up citron
½ c. raisins
1 tbs. grated candied lemon rind

Dissolve yeast in warm water. Beat in rest of ingredients. Let rise in greased bowl till double in bulk (1½ hr.) Punch down and knead at least 7 min. Form in- to an oval of about 12 x 18". Fold the long way. Brush with slightly beaten egg. white mixed with 1 tbs. water. Let rise till double (60 min). Bake for 35 min. or till golden brown. Dust with confectioners' sugar or brush with icing.

ICING:

1½ c. confectioners' sugar
1½ tbs. milk. Mix with fork till smooth.

Nürnberger Lebkuchen

1 c. honey
3/4 c. brown sugar packed
1 egg
1 tsp. lemon juice
1 tsp. lemon rind, grated
2 3/4 c. flour
1½ tsp. soda
1 tsp. cinnamon
½ tsp. allspice
½ tsp. nutmeg
¼ tsp. cloves
½ c. cut up citron
½ c. chopped nuts
candied cherrie halves
blanched almond halves
glazing icing

Heat honey and sugar till dissolved.
Cool. Add egg, lemon juice, and rind.
Add mixture of flour, soda and spices.
Stir in citron and nuts. Cover with
Saran-wrap and chill overnight. Roll
out ¼" thick. Cut in rounds and decorate
with cherries and almond halves. Bake
10-12 minutes at 400°. Immediately
brush with icing and remove from cookie
sheet to cool.

ICING:
Boil 1 c. sugar and ½ c. water till syrup
(230°). Remove from heat and stir in ¼c.
confectioners' sugar. Brush hot icing on
hot cookies. (If icing gets sugary, re-
heat slightly, adding a little water until
clear.)

Marzipan Candy

8 oz. almond paste
2/3 c. marshmallow creme
2 tbs. light corn syrup
½ c. powdered sugar.

Blend all ingredients together. Knead well
and form into shapes of different fruits,
potatoes, peas in a pod and little pigs.
Brush with food coloring, roll potatoes in a little cocoa. Coloring may also be mixed with
dough to color all the way through.

127

Special Dishes
for a German Christmas Dinner

by Hannalori Gerdes

Potato balls

1 egg
3 c. cold cooked potatoes put
 through a potato ricer or food
 mill.
½ c. corn starch
1 tsp. salt
¼ tsp. baking powder
2 c. croutons made by cutting
 slices of day old bread into
 little squares and browning in
 butter.

Combine potato, salt, egg, baking powder and enough corn starch
to make a dough easily handled to
make balls. Take five or six croutons and form potato around these to
make a ball about 3" in diameter. Drop
in hard rolling boil water that is
lightly salted. Put on lid and
cook till ball floats. Only cook
a few at a time. Serve on platter
with roast pork or beef and gravy.

Stuffing for Goose

4c. white bread, cubed
8 oz. thick sliced bacon, cut in
 pieces and fried
1 c. butter
3-4 eggs
1 tsp. nutmeg
½ c. chopped parsley
1 tsp. salt
2 c. milk
1 c. chopped chestnuts (optional)

Blend ingredients and stuff goose.

Vanilla Crescents

2 sticks unsalted butter or margarine
1/3 c. sugar
1 3/4 c. flour
2/3 c. finely ground filberts or almonds
1 tsp. vanilla

Knead together and form crescents.
Bake on greased baking sheet at 350°
till lightly browned. Remove from
sheet while warm and roll in powdered sugar mixed with vanilla
sugar.

Lemon Slices

2 c. unsalted butter or margarine
2 c. powdered sugar
3 c. flour
2 eggs
grated rind from 1 lemon
juice from 1 lemon

Blend flour and butter. Add 1 c.
powdered sugar, lemon peel and two
egg yolks. Blend and then let
rest 10 min. Roll out using powdered sugar on board--no flour.
Cut in ½ moon shapes. Bake at 350°
until light brown. Make frosting
of lemon juice and remaining powdered sugar.

German Advent Wreath Stand

Put two circles of 5/8" plywood, 1/16" diameter. Drill 5/8" hole in the center of each one. Line up holes, glue and nail together.

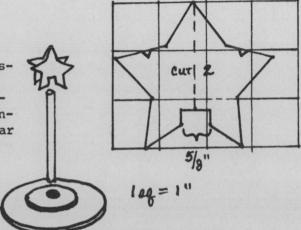

Cut 2

5/8"

1 leg = 1"

Cut out two stars of 3/8" plywood using grid pattern. Cut one star in half on the dotted line and glue pieces to whole star making it two dimensional. Dry and sand edges. Fit star down on one end of a piece of 5/8" dowel - 16" long and glue securely. Glue other end of dowel into base. Notch star as pattern shows for holding ribbon.
Wooden stand may be stained and varnished or painted red or white.

Make a wreath of spruce or pine branches over 12" diameter circular wire. Wrap branches with fine wire until wreath is nice and thick and even all around. Wrap wreath in four places, evenly spaced with red ribbon and make a loop of red ribbon for each of the four places to hang from the star. The wreath should hang about 6" above the table. Purchase little candle holders that are on spikes to insert in wreath or carve them from balsa or soft pine. Insert four red candles in holders and hang with ribbon. Added bows of red ribbon may be added also.

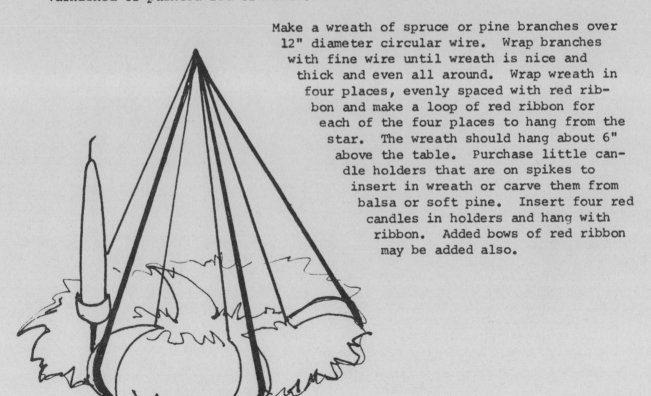

Pot Holder: Cut pieces from contrasting colors, such as a print for chicken shape and plain color for the circles. Open the circles and put cotton or polyester batting between. Quilt with machine in about 1" squares. Sew top of chicken around head, between notches.

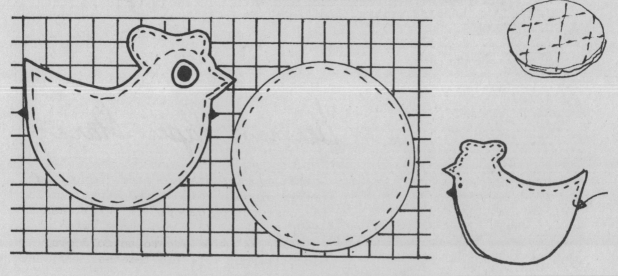

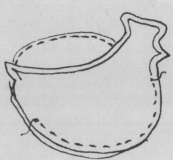

Put right side of quilted circle and right side of chicken together and stitch on machine all around except for 2½" on one side near the tail (see diagram).

Turn right side out and stitch in comb. Stuff head and tail, then overcast opening shut. Satin stitch in eyes and beak with embroidery floss. Tack holder together below beak so chicken will hold its shape.

130

Key rack

Directions for making key rack:
Cut out pattern using 3/8" plywood
with sabre or jig saw. Sand, stain
desired color or antique. Varnish
with satin varnish and paint floral
design with acrylic paints. Add
brass hooks.

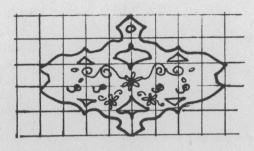

1 sq. = 2"

German Paper Stars

German paper stars are made from either
silver or gold foil or red paper similar
to construction paper. You will need a
strip of paper 22" long and 3" wide.
Fold in 3/4" wide accordian fold over
block(1); cut (2); tie together (3); and
glue (4).

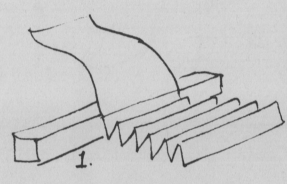

1.

2.

3.

GLUE

4.

Christmas in Sweden begins
late in November with many
preparations, things to cook,
festivities to plan, ornaments and gifts to make for
this most joyful and precious
holiday.

I remember my Grandmother ordering
salted lutefisk (a special white fish)
from Sweden very early in October so she
would be sure to have it by December 9 when
soaking the delicacy needed to begin. It was
one dish that is a must for our midnight
smorgasbord on Christmas eve. Now lutefisk
can be purchased already soaked and frozen
ready to be cooked.

St. Lucia Day, a special Swedish tradition, is cele-
brated on December 13. It is adapted from a pagan holiday celebrating the
return of more hours of daylight to the dark Swedish winter. In each household, the oldest daughter plays the part of St. Lucia. She rises very early
in the morning, puts on a white dress and a crown of evergreen topped by
seven lighted candles. She serves her family hot coffee and St. Lucia buns
while they are still in bed.

Christmas eve in our family is celebrated by attending church services early
in the evening, them gathering together at Grandmother's home for smorgasbord
at midnight. Dishes of home made cheeses, Christmas breads, brown beans,
lutefisk and boiled potatoes, pickled herring, ham, meatballs, special ginger
and almond cookies, fruit soup, much hot coffee and so many little goodies
it is difficult to name them all.

Christmas celebrations in Sweden
continue until the twelfth night,
January 6, when the visit of the
wisemen is commemorated. This is
a time of carol singing and gift
giving. Every Swedish gift
no matter
how small,
is wrapped
in snowy white
non-glazed paper
and sealed with
red sealing wax.
The smell of sealing
wax recalls the holiday
season to Swedish people all
their lives.

The Swedes are very im-
aginative and create
beautiful decorations of
simple design in straw,
wood, metal and glass from
ornaments to special cookies
that are made to resemble stars,
angels, reindeer, birds, nativity
figures and ginger houses among
others.

Enclosed are sketches and instructions for making straw ornaments, a pattern for a Christmas gingerbread house made from Luciapepparkakor (Lucia Ginger snaps), cookie patterns, a bread board, a recipe for St. Lucia buns, Swedish fruit soup, and my own recipe for limpa (Swedish Christmas rye bread).

An excellent book of Swedish cooking is FAVORITE SWEDISH RECIPES, edited by Sam Widenfelt, Dover Pub., Inc. This is an unabridged republication of the original Swedish Food, published by Esseltes Goteborginsindustrier AB. It has both Swedish and English indexes of food.

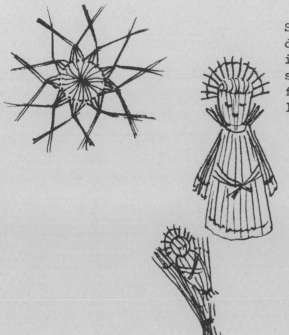

Straw ornaments should be 6" to 8" in diameter. Choose bright colored straw in pieces 12 to 14 inches in length. The straw may be woven with embroidery floss, fine ribbon or sew with thread. Fasten little loops for hanging the ornaments.

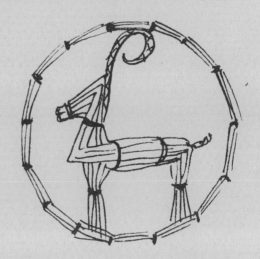

Bread Board

MATERIALS: One 1" thick board of finely grained pine or maple, 10" by 20", a coping or sabre saw, ½ pt. gym floor varnish or other water proof varnish and acrylic paints for decoration.

Cut shape from board. Use an electric drill to cut hole in the handle. Sand all edges and entire board very smooth. Paint pattern on one side with acrylic paint. When dry, seal with 2 coats of the varnish on the painted side only. Do not varnish the edges or the back side of the board. The untreated side can be used for a cutting board and the decorated side hung forward on the wall as a decoration.

1 sq = 2"

133

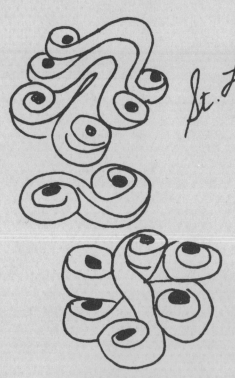

St. Lucia saffron buns

1 c. butter or margarine
1 c. sugar
1 c. boiling water
1 tsp. salt
1 tsp. ground saffron

Mix the above and stir until shortening melts.
Cook until lukewarm.

Dissolve 2 pkg. yeast in ½ c. warm water.

Add 1 beaten egg
     2/3 c. milk

Add 4 c. all purpose flour, beat until smooth.

Add ½ c. currents or raisins and remaining 4 c.
flour. Put in greased bowl, cover with damp
towel and let rise until double (2 hrs.).

Turn on floured board and knead until smooth. Divide into portions and make
ropes of dough to form buns similar to the illustration. Use raisins for
decoration.

Place on greased baking sheets, cover and let rise. Brush with slightly beaten
egg, sprinkle with sugar and bake in 425° F. oven for 5 to 10 minutes.
(Saffron coffee bread may be made from the same recipe. Form dough into braids
and sprinkle with chopped almonds and sugar just before baking.)

Limpa   (Christmas rye bread)

3¼ c. rye glour
2½ c. all purpose flour
½ c. warm water with 2 pkg. yeast dissolved in it.

Combine ½ c. lukewarm milk
        2 tbs. sugar
        1 tbs. salt and stir to dissolve.

Beat in ½ c. molasses
        2 tbs. shortening
        yeast mixture
        2 tbs. finely chopped orange rind

Add flour and beat mixture until dough leaves the sides of the bowl. Turn
onto floured board and knead until smooth and elastic. Let rise in greased
bowl until double. Divide into 2 portions, shape into round loaves. Place
on well greased cookie sheet. Let rise until double. Bake at 375° F. for
30 to 35 minutes. Remove from baking sheet and brush with butter. Makes
2 loaves.

Luciapepparkakor

1 c. butter or margarine
2½ c. brown sugar
½ c. milk
1¼ c. molasses
1 tbs. ginger
1 tbs. lemon rind
2 tbs. baking soda
9 c. flour

Combine all ingredients except flour. Stir for 10 minutes. Add flour and work until smooth. Cover and chill overnight.

For ginger bread house, cut patterns from heavy paper on cardboard. Roll dough out thin on large greased cookie sheet. Lay pattern over and out around using sharp knife. Brush with water and bake at 300° F. for 12 to 14 minutes. Loosen from cookie sheet and when cool, join pieces by dipping edges in sugar melted in a saucepan or use confectioners sugar frosting in decorator tube to secure joints and to decorate house.

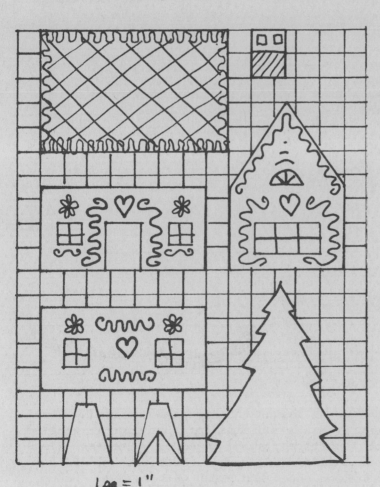

1 sq = 1"

Decorator frosting

1 c. confectioners sugar.
1 egg white

Beat together until smooth and force through a pastry tube with a fine point.

To make cookies, roll dough thin on lightly floured board. Make patterns from cardboard and cut around the patterns with a sharp knife. Bake cookies on a greased cookie sheet in 300° F. oven for 12 minutes. Decorate with icing when cool. These cookies are very crisp and spicy. (If you wish to make a softer cookie, use only 6 c. flour instead of 9 and be sure dough is well chilled before rolling it out.)

Cookie patterns

MISSE

NASSE

1 sq = 1/2"

Fruit soup

Cook together:

½ lb. dried prunes
½ lb. white raisins
1 lb. dried mixed fruit (pears,
    peaches, apples)
1 sliced lemon
2 c. sugar
2 cinnamon sticks
2 tbs. cornstarch

Put in large pan, cover with water
and simmer until the fruit is done.
Chill.

Serve with Christmas cookies and
lots of hot coffee.

Drömmar

(Dream cookies)

1 c. butter
3/4 c. sugar
2 tsp. vanilla
1 tsp. baking powder
2 c. flour
35 blanched almonds

Brown butter slightly and pur into
bowl. Cool. Add sugar and stir until
fluffy. Add vanilla, then flour and
baking powder sifted together. Work
dough until smooth. Roll into 70 little
balls. Place on buttered cookie sheet
with half an almond on top of each.
Bake at 250° F. until golden brown
(about 25 minutes).

136

Layette night

Along with the ancient custom of burning the
yule log at Christmas, some French families
observe the tradition of layette night.
An evening before Christmas is reserved for
all the family to help make a layette of clothes for
a new born child. On Christmas eve the layette is left
on the doorstep of the home of a needy family with a new
baby. The gift is always left anonymously.

This loving tradition would be a good one for families or church fellowships to adopt in their celebration of Christ's birthday.

Following are patterns for a baby layette that is simple to make using
flannel, cotton and yarn. Also a recipe for French Christmas onion soup,
French herb bread and the Buche de Noel or yule log (a traditional French
Christmas dessert).

MATERIALS: For sleeper; 1 5/8 yd. flannel, cotton knit
   or terry cloth, 39" width. One 16" zipper
   and bias tape.

   Hood; 3/8 yd. cotton fabric, 3/8 yd
   lining material, 16" piece of 3"
   ribbon for binding, ½ yd. of ½"
   ribbon for drawstring.

   Blanket; 1½ yd. 45" cotton or
   quilted nylon material, 1½ yd.
   45" cotton flannel for backing
   and polyester quilt fill.
   You will also need 6 yd. bias tape.

   You may wish to make the blanket
   top by patching 8" squares together.
   Use ½" seam.   You will need
   56 of these squares. Sew
   together with machine in strips
   containing eight squares, then sew
   strips together.

To make the blanket, pin the flannel to a quilting frame, wrong side up.
Put the polyester fill on top of the flannel and then the blanket top, right
side up on top of this. Pin in place. Tie with colored yarn on the corners
of each square and one in the middle. For plain blanket, you will have to
mark the squares lightly with pencil so your ties will be even. Bind edges
with bias tape.

137

You can make a simple quilting frame if
you do not have one, from four pieces of 1" by 2"
pine lumber, 65" long. Tack folded strips of
heavy cotton fabric, such as duck, to
the wood and use "C" clamps to
fasten frame together at the corners.

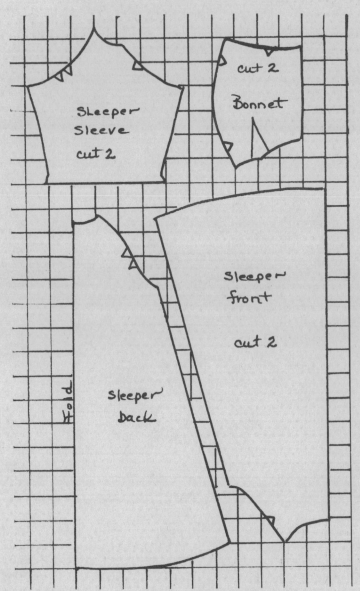

SLEEPER: Match knotches
on sleeve to front and back pieces.
Sew 5/8" seam with right sides
together. Sew seam from bottom
of front to knotch. **Baste rest**
of seam and sew in zipper according to package instructions.

Sew seam from sleeve edge to
bottom of garment. Sew bottom
of garment together. Face
neckline with bias tape. (Casing
may be put in neck to run ribbon
through for a neck tie if you wish.)
Finish sleeves by making an inch
hem. Ties may also be used in
sleeves if you wish.

BONNET: Stitch dart. Join knotches
and sew 5/8" seam. Make lining
the same. With right sides together, stitch neckline of hood
and lining together. Turn and
top stitch 5/8" to make casing
for ribbon ties. Bind front of
bonnet with the 3" ribbon as you
would a blanket. Finish bottom
edge of ribbon so that ties may be
inserted in casing at the neck.

Christmas Onion Soup

Cook about 10 minutes until tender but not brown;
    2 large onions, sliced and separated
    2 tbs. margarine

Sprinkle with 1 tbs. flour. Stir until blended.

Add 1 qt. milk, cover and simmer 20 minutes. Add 1 tsp. salt
and a dash of pepper.

Stir a small amount of hot soup into 2 beaten egg yolks, stirring until blended. Return egg mixture to soup, stirring until
blended. Season to taste. Sprinkle each serving with grated
parmesan cheese. Serve with French herb bread. Serves 8.

French herb Bread

Combine in large bowl:
    2 pkt. dry yeast
    2 tbs. sugar
    1 tsp. salt
    1½ c. flour

Heat in saucepan until warm:
    1 c. milk
    1 tbs. vinegar
    ¼ c. water
    ¼ c. margarine

Add liquid to flour mixture and blend on low speed of mixer until moistened.
Beat 3 minutes at medium speed.

Stir in 1½ c. additional flour to form a sticky dough. Knead on floured
surface adding ½ to 1 c. flour until dough is smooth and pliable. Place in
greased bowl and let rise until double.

Punch down dough and roll into rectangle shape, 16" by 8". Spread with the
following filling.

    ½ c. minced onion   1 tbs. minced parsley
    1 clove garlic, minced   2 tbs. margarine
    ½ tsp. salt

Heat in saucepan until butter is melted, spread on dough and roll dough
tightly, like a jelly roll.

Place seam side down on greased cookie sheet and let rise until double.

Bake at 400° F. until golden brown (20 to 30 minutes). Brush with butter
after baking and sprinkle with parsley.

139

Buche de Noël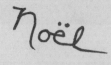

Sift together: 1 c. flour
      1 tsp. baking powder
      ¼ tsp. salt

Beat 3 eggs at high speed on mixer until thick and light. Beat in 1 c. sugar a few tablespoons at a time. Beat until very thick.

Blend in ¼ c. water and 1 tbs. lemon juice.

Gently fold dry ingredients into egg mixture. Spread evenly on 10" by 15" jelly roll pan that is lined with lightly greased waxed paper.

Bake 12 to 15 minutes at 375° F. until cake springs back when lightly touched. Turn on towel that is sprinkled with confectioners sugar. Remove wax paper. Roll up cake and towel from the short side. Cool on rack.

CHOCOLATE FILLING: Cream together
½ c. soft margarine, 3/4 c. confectioners
sugar. Add 3 sq. melted chocolate that
has been cooled, 1 tsp. salt, 2 tsp.
instant coffee, 1 tsp. vanilla.

Beat 3 egg whites very stiff. Gradually
add 1¼ c. sifted powdered sugar. Add
chocolate mixture.

Spread one half of mixture on jelly roll. Roll up, and decorate the outside with remaining filling that has been put in a pastry tube with a star tip. Make long strips of the filling to make the cake look like a log. Garnish with meringue mushrooms and sprinkle with chopped nuts.

Meringue Mushrooms

Beat 1 egg white with a dash of cream of tartar until foamy. Beat in ¼ c. sugar gradually and beat until stiff, glossy peaks form.

Spoon into pastry bag with large round tip.
Hold bag close to greased and floured cookie
sheet. Press out 3/4" wide cap. Smooth
top if it is peaked.

For stems, hold bag vertically, pull
straight up until short stem forms.

Bake for 30 to 40 minutes or until dry
and ivory colored in 250° F. oven.
Loosen with spatula and cool on rack.
Make a small hole in the underside
of cap. Put in a little thick frosting
made of 2 tbs. butter, ½ c. confectioners
sugar and a drop or two of water. Insert
pointed end of stem.

140

Festival of Lights

Part of our heritage as Christians are the religious holidays of the Jews. Hanukkah is a Jewish holiday that falls near Christmas time. It commemorates the victory of the Jewish community over Antiochus who had closed all the houses of worship.

Hanukkah is a festival of light in the dark days of early winter. It is a time of small gift giving and celebration and it's legend is pleasant.

Hanukkah began several thousand years ago when the Jews had no independant kingdom. They were split in many groups, making it easy for the temples to be closed by Antiochus. After several years, Judah Maccabeus and his brothers united the Jews and in a victorious battle restored the temples. Legend has it that there was just enough oil to keep the lamp on the ark of the covenant burning one night, but it miraculously lasted for eight days and eight nights.

To celebrate the memory of the restoration of the houses of worship, the menorah (a nine branch candlestick) is lighted in the home. On the first night a special candle called the shammash is lighted and used to light one other candle. Each night for the next seven days the shammash is used to light another candle until on the eighth night all nine are lighted. On one or more nights small presents are exchanged by family members. There are also some special foods that are served for the celebration. Included are some of these special recipes.

Potato Latkes

4 large potatoes and 1 medium onion, peeled and grated
Add 2 well beaten eggs and stir to blend

Stir in ½ c. all purpose flour and 1 tsp. salt gradually.

Heat shortening or oil to 1" depth in a large skillet. Drop batter by large spoonfuls into hot shortening. Fry until golden brown, turn, brown second side. Drain on paper towels. Serve with hot applesauce.

141

Filled doughnuts

(to be served with a dairy meal)

1 pkg. yeast in ¼ c, warm water (110°)
1 c. milk heated until warm with
3 tbs. shortening
1/3 c. sugar
1½ tsp. salt

Stir in 1 beaten egg, grated rind
of 1 lemon or 1 orange and 1 tsp.
vanilla.

Cool until lukewarm.

Combine yeast and milk mixtures.
Gradually add 4 c. flour. Knead
on floured board until smooth.
Cover, let rise in warm place about 1 hr.
or until doubled in bulk. Punch down.
Roll out on floured board to ¼"
thickness. Cut in 2½" circles. Top
circles with small spoonfuls of prune
jam. Top with another circle.
Moisten edges with water and press
edges together. Cover, let rise until
double. Fry in deep fat (375° F.) until
golden brown on each side. Drain on
paper towels and sprinkle with confectioners sugar. Makes 1½ dozen.

Sweet potato Kugelach

4 c. mashed potatoes
3 eggs well beaten
½ c. honey
1/3 c. rendered chicken fat
½ c. water
1 tsp. salt
2 tbs. lemon juice
2 tsp. lemon or orange rind

Combine all ingredients and
blend well. Spoon mixture
into greased muffin tins,
filling cups 2/3 full. Bake
30 minutes at 350° F. Serve
hot with chicken. 6 to 8
servings.

Sesame - Honey candy

2 c. sugar
½ tsp. ground ginger
2/3 c. honey
dash salt
½ c. sesame seed, toasted
2/3 c. chopped walnuts

Combine sugar, honey, ginger, salt in medium saucepan. Cook and stir over
low heat until mixture boils. Cook 8 minutes more, stirring occasionally.
Remove from heat. Stir in sesame seeds and nuts. Pour into greased shallow
pan. Cool slightly. Butter or oil hands and press and spread candy very
thin, working quickly. Cut into diamond shaped pieces with scissors while
still warm. Makes 6 dozen pieces.

142

Christmas in Nigeria is an exciting, festive day. Early in the morning people put on their new clothes and admire each other's new outfits. Some families may have tea and kwasi (fried bean cakes) before going to church or some designated area for the Nativity drama, instituted by early missionaries.

This Christmas morning drama is a long and elaborate production including many actors and scenes. The audience follows the whole Bible story of Christ's beginnings. It starts with Mary being told by the angel that she is to be the mother of Jesus, to her marriage with Joseph, the trip to Bethlehem, the searching for a room at many inns, and finally being able to sleep in the stable. Then Jesus is born and a star appears. An angel comes to the shepherds to tell them of the birth of Jesus and they are so-o-o (the Nigerians always turn this into comedy) afraid. The wisemen are told of the birth and go by Herod's palace to ask for directions to the birthplace. The audience appreciates Herod's guile as he asks the wisemen to return and tell him where they find the new king so that he may worship him. The drama may go on for a couple of hours. But the Nigerians love dramas so this is no problem.

Unlike our idea of a play, Nigerian "dramas" have no set script, and the Christmas drama is no exception. Lines are all ad libbed and there is considerable over-acting and up-staging.

Christmas for Nigerians is a time when every family has something special to eat. Instead of the usual guinea corn mush, all who can afford it have rice and add meat to the soup. In the afternoon the children may go caroling at homes of the wealthier neighbors, in anticipation of candy or cookies.(Much in the spirit of our Hallowe'en trick-or-treating, some children make and wear masks.)

Christmas is also a time to return home from the city. Each village bulges with relatives and friends who have returned for the holidays. In the afternoon the traditional dance begins near the chief's compound. It continues on into the night, even until dawn. Everyone participates, grandparents, mothers and fathers, young folk, children. Even babies tied on their mothers' backs, join in the fun. Recent years have seen a gradual shift toward Christmas becoming a community celebration and homecoming that involves Moslems as well as Christians in all the activities. This is made easier by the incorporation of traditional elements of long-standing pagan and Moslem celebrations, new clothes, feasting and dancing, that all in the community can identify with.

Nigeria

by Margaret Thomason

143

Following are recipes for the traditional Nigerian meat soup, a treat in the form of sugared ground nuts and instructions on how to make a Nigerian tie-dye shirt.

Nigerian meat soup

¼ c. oil
1 lb. meat, cubed
2 c. water
1 onion, chopped
1 small can tomato paste
red pepper or Tobasco sauce
    to taste
salt

Brown meat in oil. Add 1 c. water and simmer 45 minutes or until tender. Add tomato paste, onion, pepper, salt and remaining water. Cover and simmer 25 minutes.

Variations: Chicken can be used. Disjoint and cook in water until tender. Follow the rest as above.

Serve soup over rice or a very thick cornmeal mush.

Sugared ground nuts

1 c. water
2 c. sugar
4 to 6 c. shelled peanuts

Dissolve sugar in water. Add peanuts. Boil slowly and stir frequently until sugar crystalizes on the peanuts. Spread on cookie sheet to dry.

African tie-dye shirt

Tie-dye is a craft of the African people and garments that are made are simple but have very attractive lines. If you would like to make a different kind of gift, try this African shirt and dye it yourself. No hems at the neck or bottom. The fringed edges are desired.

MATERIALS: 1¼ yds. of 36" wide cotton broadcloth or unbleached muslin. Machine wash in hot water and bleach. Wash twice more to remove all sizing and bleach. Dry and iron.

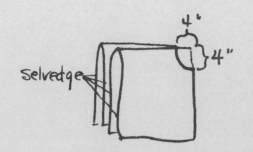

Fold fabric in half, putting raw edges together. Fold again in half so selvedges are
together (see diagram). Cut 8" diameter
circle for the neck.

Open half way and tie with cotton cord.
Pull tight. Try different ways of tieing.

Prepare dye bath of desired colors
using ½ the water recommended in
package directions. Add 1 tbs.
salt to each dye bath. Make sure
dye baths are very hot. Dip tied
fabric in dye a section at a time.
allowing dye to penetrate. Blot
excess dye off with paper towels
between each color change.

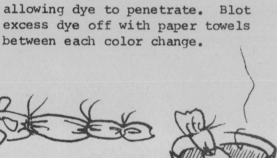

Blot and remove strings quickly. Hang on the line until
nearly dry. Put through repeated baths of cold salt water
until water is clear. Press fabric and fold again.

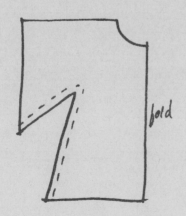

Make a pattern of newsprint that will
fit around hips and comfortable under
arms like diagram. Place pattern on
fabric and cut. Sew up under arm
seams and press. Turn right side out.
Press and your shirt is done. It is
wash fast and very servicable.

145

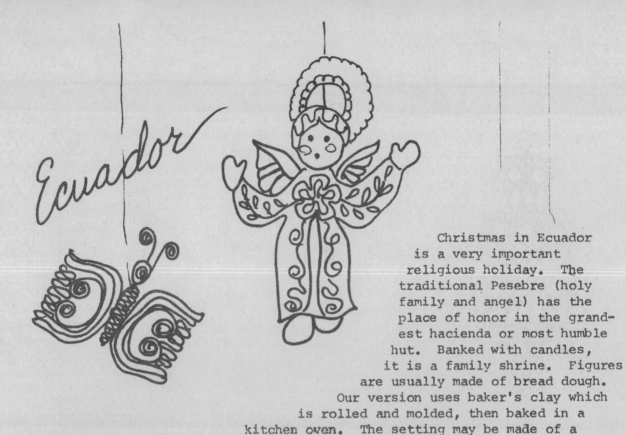

Ecuador

Christmas in Ecuador
is a very important
religious holiday. The
traditional Pesebre (holy
family and angel) has the
place of honor in the grand-
est hacienda or most humble
hut. Banked with candles,
it is a family shrine. Figures
are usually made of bread dough.
Our version uses baker's clay which
is rolled and molded, then baked in a
kitchen oven. The setting may be made of a
cardboard box with primitive designs of poster paint.

As in Mexico, Christmas eve is celebrated in worship at midnight.
Sometimes processions of candle or torch bearers guide the way.

On December 17, a day honoring the Virgin of Solitude, puffy anise
flavored doughnuts called bunuelos are served. Customers
buy plates of bunuelos from street vendors and smash the
plates on the ground after eating the tasty little
doughnuts.

Almond empanaditas, a crimped, deep fried pastry with
almond cinnamon filling is also a favorite treat served
with coffee during the Christmas season.

The Ecuadorian Indians are amazing artists. They
make detailed pottery, bold jewelry and beautiful
weavings of vivid primitive colors and designs.
You may want to create a weaving such as the
one included for a gift or wall decoration for
your home. Beautiful gifts from Ecuador are
available for purchase through SERRV.

Instruction for making a Pesebre and bread
dough ornaments are printed in the creche
section of this book.

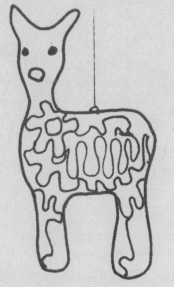

146

Star weaving

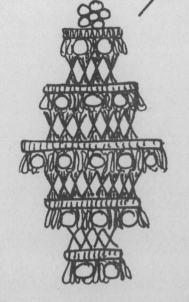

MATERIALS: Five pieces of inch doweling cut lengths of one piece 24", two 18", two 9". 2/3 yd. dark green burlap, 1 skein each of bright pink and bright orange yarn (medium weight), 5 skeins lime green rug yarn.

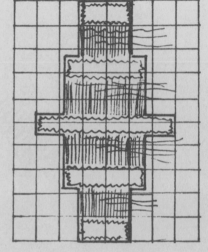

Cut burlap in shape according to diagram. Sew with zig-zag stitch on machine to secure the 4" areas. Pull threads in 5" areas as diagram shows. Tie pulled areas in sections.

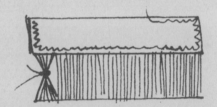

Make loops of rug yarn on dowel sticks so that the loops hang down 5" (see diagram). Glue yarn at ends to secure and paint ends of dowels green to match yarn.

Secure dowels firmly to top edge of each solid strip with heavy green thread.

Make a tab for top of hanging from a piece of dark green burlap 4" by 8". Fold and stitch on two sides (see diagram). Turn inside out and sew raw edge securely to top center of hanging.

2½"
for large
1½"
for small pom-poms

Make pink and orange pom-poms to be fastened to hanging. You will need 5 large pink, 10 large orange, 5 small pink, 1 small orange.

To make pom-poms, wind yarn on heavy cardboard form pictured in diagram. Tie securely in center. Cut yarn at top and bottom.

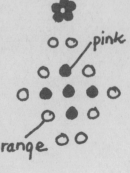

pink

orange

Trim to make puffy ball. Sew pom-poms to hanging following the pattern above. Attach plastic curtain ring to center back of the tab at the top of the hanging.

Bunuelos

4 tbs. butter
3/4 c. milk
1 tbs. aniseed

Heat in saucepan to boiling. Cool.
Stir in 2 beaten eggs.

Sift together 3 c. flour
    1 tsp. baking powder
    1 tsp. salt

Add egg mixture to dry ingredients and
knead dough on a lightly floured board
until smooth. Shape into 20 little balls.
Let rest 5 minutes. Roll each ball into a
4" circle. Fry in deep fat (375° F.) for
4 minutes, turning once. Drain on paper towel.

Combine ½ c. sugar and 1 tsp. ground cinnamon in
a paper bag. Shake doughnuts in sugar mixture. Makes 20.

Almond Empanaditas

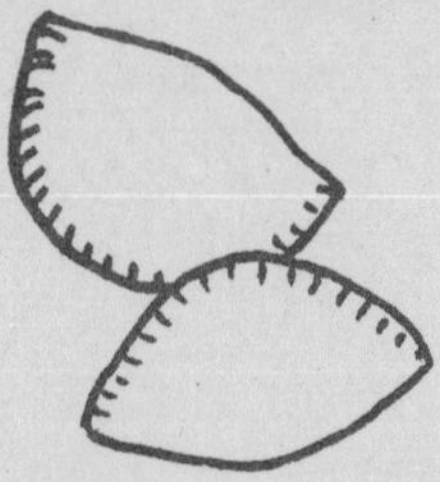

2 c. sifted all purpose flour
1 tsp. salt
2 tsp. baking powder
½ c. shortening
½ to 2/3 c. ice water
3/4 c. chopped blanched almonds
½ c. sugar
1 tsp. ground cinnamon
1 egg white
¼ tsp. almond extract

Sift flour, salt and baking powder together. Cut in shortening until
mixture resembles coarse crumbs. Add ice water 1 tbs. at a time until all
flour is moistened. Shape into ball. Roll out on lightly floured surface
1/8" thick. Cut into 2½" circles. Mix together almonds, sugar and cinnamon.
Beat egg white and extract until frothy. Stir in almond mixture. Place 1 tsp.
of almond filling on half of each circle of dough. Wet edges and fold over
dough and seal with tines of a fork. Fry in hot fat (375° F.) about 4 minutes
until golden brown, turning once. Drain on paper toweling. Makes 3 dozen.

Christmas south of the border

Navidad is a colorful celebration of the birth of Christ. Much color and pageantry accompany festivities in a carnival fashion. Children don't know who Santa Claus is. It may be "El Nino Jesus" who brings gifts on Christmas day, or the three wisemen whose arrival time is the twelfth night.

A giant creche or nacimiento occupies the center of the city plaza as well as each home. A pinata swings from every rooftop ready to burst with candy and prizes on Christmas day. Little birds' nests, Ojo's and ornaments of bright yarn are also used to decorate.

The Mexican pinata was originally an earthenware jug disguised as an animal, a person or some curious object, then filled with toys and sweets. Blindfolded children break the hanging pinata with sticks. They keep whatever they can pick up.

Christmas eve is celebrated by a candlelight procession to the church for worship at midnight.

In recent years Mexican folk art emphasizing madonnas and wisemen has attracted collectors the world over. Craftsmen use plaster, fabrics of various kinds, crude clay, wood and yarn.

We include recipes for a Mexican Christmas eve salad, Christmas pudding, plans to make a pinata, an Ojo and little birds' nests for Christmas tree decorations or favors.

Christmas eve salad

Arrange the following fruits and vegetables on a lettuce lined platter.

1 banana and 2 apples cliced (sprinkle with lemon juice to prevent darkening).
1 c. sliced beets, drained
2 c. pineapple chunks, drained
½ c. spanish peanuts sprinkled over fruits and beets.
pomegranate seeds, if available.

Serve mayonnaise or salad dressing thinned with a little milk as a dressing for the salad. Serves 6 to 8.

149

Budin de Navidad

2 envelopes unflavored gelatin
1 c. sugar
2 c. milk
3 eggs
2 c. whipped cream or dream whip
1 tsp. almond extract
¼ tsp. vanilla
3 drops each of red and green
  food coloring
custard sauce

Mix gelatin, ½ c. sugar and milk in sauce-pan. Heat until gelatin dissolves. Chill until slightly thickened. Separate eggs and beat whites until foamy. Add ½ c. sugar 1 tbs. at a time until meringue stands in firm peaks. Fold meringue and whipped cream into thickened gelatin. Fold in almond extract and vanilla. Divide mixture in thirds. Fold red coloring into one, green into another and leave remainder white. Spoon green mixture into 6 c. mold. Top with white mixture and then red. Chill 4 hours. Serve with custard sauce.

CUSTARD SAUCE: Beat 3 egg yolks slightly in top of double boiler. Beat in ¼ c. sugar, dash salt, 1½ c. milk. Cook, stirring constantly over simmering water until custard thickens and coats a metal spoon. Stir in 1 tsp. vanilla. Strain into a small bowl and chill. Makes 1 3/4 c.

Ojo
(God's Eye)

MATERIALS: One 1/8" dowel stick 30", one 20", and two 5". Yarn in a variety of colors and white glue.

To begin, hold crossed 2 larger dowels in cross formation bisecting at the center of each piece. Hold in left hand. Wind yarn over and around each stick, working out from center (see drawing). Work either clockwise or counter-clockwise, whichever is easier. To change from one color to another, make a knot, covering ends as you wind the yarn. If you wish spaces between strands, wrap around each dowel twice as you proceed. Finish with a knot and a drop of glue to hold the yarn to the dowel. Trim ends of dowels with pom-poms or tassels made of yarn.

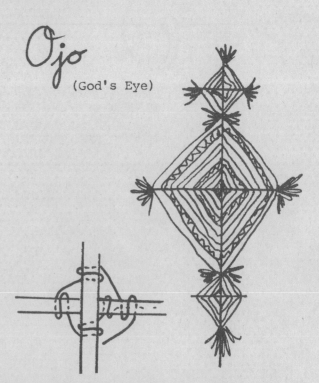

Variation: Start two Ojo's with single crossed sticks 20" in length. Weave about 1½" centers on each of contrasting colors. Put the two Ojo's together to make an eight sided, two dimensional design. Begin weaving the two as one. Change colors and reverse the weaving technique every so often to give depth.

Piñata

Blow up a round balloon to about 12"
diameter. Wrap very heavily with strips
of newsprint that has been dipped in a
solution of 3 parts wallpaper paste,
1 part white glue and 3 parts water.
This should be a rather thin consistency.
Make the papier-mache at least ¼"thick
over the balloon. Let dry. Release air
from balloon and fill the cavity with
candy and prizes. Tie a heavy string
around the papier-mache ball and tape it
to the ball with masking tape. Leave a generous loop at the top for hanging.

To decorate the pinata to look like a chicken, make
a second smaller ball of papier-mache or use a large
styrofoam ball that is trimmed so that it will glue
to the larger ball. Form the tail with one full
circle and ½ circle of light weight cardboard (see
diagram). Cut ½ circle to body shape and slit edges
of cardboard so that cardboard will fit to ball. Add
a small cone to head for the beak and a shaped piece of
cardboard to make comb and waddle.
Fasten to papier-mache with wide masking tape.

Cover waddle, comb and beak with several
layers of colored tissue paper using
white glue. Cut strips of brilliant
colored tissue paper 4" wide. Fold
in half lengthwise and cut 1½"
slashes along folded edge.

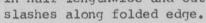

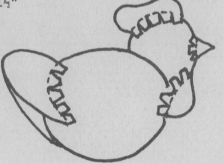

Start fastening tissue strips at the end of the tail.
Glue and wind, overlapping just a bit until entire
body is covered to where the head fastens to the
body. Then begin winding in a circle on one side
of the head, from the outer edge, working in to
where the eye should be. Repeat on the other side
of the head. Now entire head and body are covered
with bright colored tissue. Use a little circle of
black paper for the eye.

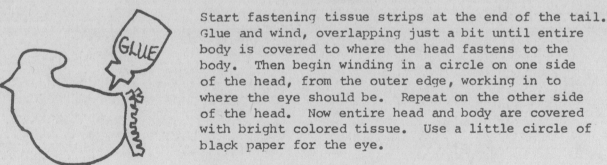

Floopy feet are made of lightweight cardboard with several
layers of tissue paper glued to it, collage fashion.
These feet may be glued or wired to bottom of chicken.

151

Bird's nest ornament

MATERIALS: Wallpaper paste, white glue, excelsior or chopped straw, empty spray can lid or ½ leggs plastic egg, one snap clothespin for each nest you intend to make as a tree decoration.

Make a solution of one part wallpaper paste mixed with water to package directions, to one part white glue in a deep bowl. Submerge one handful of straw or excelsior into mixture, then squeeze out excess paste. Mold straw into an upside down nest shaped over lid. When it begins to set, lift off nest. Dry right side up at room temperature or dry on a cookie sheet in a low oven. Glue pinch clothespin underneath the nest to attach it to the tree.

Eggs made of little yarn balls, candy or painted papier-mache and origami or yarn covered papier-mache birds may be added to the nests.

Birds of yarn

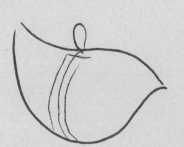

Wad piece of newsprint into a ball, 2" in diameter. Use papier-mache method for making the pinata. Wrap ball of paper with strips dipped in the paste. Mold and form as you go to sculpt a simple bird form similar to the diagram. Let dry. Tie a heavy string around the body with a loop at the top. Tape the string to the body. Glue and wrap bird with heavy bright colored yarn similar to drawing or create your own design.

Christmas in India

by Margaret Thomason

There is much preparation to be done when Christmas time in India is near. Dirt floors need to be replastered, walls are whitewashed both at church and at home, the brass is shined and all sparkling for guests, the church decorated and the Christmas drama is rehearsed.

The celebrating and preparation goes on for many days. As early as the 18th and 19th of December the mission schools have a three to four hour program. Drama, singing, and dancing are old traditions in India and all of them have been incorporated into the celebrating of Christ's birth.

The drama or pageantry begins with an angel appearing to Mary telling her that God has chosen her to be the mother of Jesus and continues with her meeting with Joseph, their trip to Bethlehem, the night of Christ's birth, the news brought to the shepherds and wisemen, and their visit. The drama is given sometimes two or three days before Christmas or it can be presented on Christmas morning or evening.

Singing is a real part of Christmas celebration in India. Many Christmas hymns are sung in church services; also after midnight on the 24th, the Christians go caroling. They enjoy going to neighboring villages to sing.

Church service on Christmas morning is a Sunday type service celebrating Christ's birth. However things look very different on this day. Everyone present has on new clothes and the church building is decorated. In the church there are many banners, palm leaves, and flowers. The walls are fresh and bright with new whitewash. After the services everyone gets an Indian sweet or candy.

Also during Christmas time there is much dancing. The Guretit dance is particularly done on festival days and the Garbbo dance, done only by women who sing and dance in a group, is done at this time.

The day after Christmas is a time of playing games, an unusual time when men and women play group games together. Other activities include outdoor sports such as ball and bicycle riding.

Between Christmas and New Year's friends usually go and visit other friends and relatives. It is a time when families are together. Every visitor is served tea and a sweet.

153

Sweets from India

by Tsun Hsien Bhagat

Coconut squares

½ c. boiling water
2 tbs. corn syrup
½ c. sugar
1½ c. brown sugar
pinch of salt
4 tbs. butter
1½ c. shredded coconut
½ tsp. cardamon powder

Add salt, corn syrup and sugar in
boiling water and cook until the
temperature reaches 238⁰ F.

Remove from heat and add butter
and coconut and cardamon.

Beat the mixture until it starts
to harden.

Quickly pour into a greased pan
and cut into squares after it is
cold.

Gulab Jaman

(Sweet milk ball in syrup)

3 c. non-fat dry milk powder
1 c. bisquick
4 tbs. butter, melted
½ c. milk

Combine and from into balls.
Fry the balls at 375⁰ F. until
brown.

In large saucepan combine
2½ c. sugar
3½ c. water
Bring to a boil and cook for 10
minutes and keep warm.

Keep balls in syrup.

Karunjis

2 pkg. or ½ fresh coconut, grated
3/4 c. sugar
1 c. raisins

1½ tsp nutmeg
1 tsp. cardamon powder

Mix all the above ingredients and let stand while making pastry.

PASTRY: 4 c. white flour
        1 c. shortening (crisco, margarine
           or butter)
        1 tsp. sugar

½ tsp baking powder
pinch of salt
3/4 c. water + 2 tbs.

Sift flour, baking powder, sugar and salt into mixing bowl. Cut in shortening
as for pie crust. Mix enough water to bind. Knead lightly on floured board.
Roll very thin and cut into 4" or 5" rounds. Put one teaspoon coconut mixture
on each round and pinch into half moons (be sure they are sealed). Fry in
deep fat until brown and drain of paper towel.

154

Crafts of Christmas

Creche

The creche originated in Italy during the Middle Ages. The idea of carved figures to commemorate the birth of Christ spread over all Europe and inspired artists of a dozen different lands to use their talents to foster the custom of the creche in homes and churches.

Simple miniatures to life sized carvings were made. Central European countries altered the size to fit into small boxes which were carried through the streets by singing children. Despite the size, creche figures maintain their spirit of gentle and devout dignity.

Today Nativity scenes may be purchased at any variety store or for great sums at antique marts of the world, but it is most meaningful when families create their own. They may be carved from soap, made of clay, bread dough, paper, fabric, wood, plaster, straw, spools, metal or glass. But no matter what the media- they still say, "Peace on earth-good will to men."

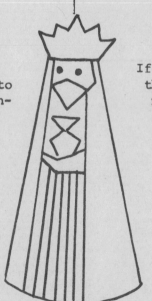

The mobile pictured on this page can be made from wood and paper. The star is created by overlapping thin flat sticks and gluing with the vertical glued on last. Then gluing it to the crossarm. The figures may be made of construction paper, beginning with basic shape and cutting patterns of different colors and gluing them in place. See diagram. Use the same pattern on both sides. After glue is dry, coat with one layer of acrylic matt varnish which can be purchased at any art or hobby store. Make a small hole in top with needle and hang by thread to crossarm. Different layers may be worked, using three or more crossarms and balancing them properly.

If you wish to copy these designs, make a grid on tracing paper of ½" squares. Lay it over this page. Copy and expand to any size you wish.

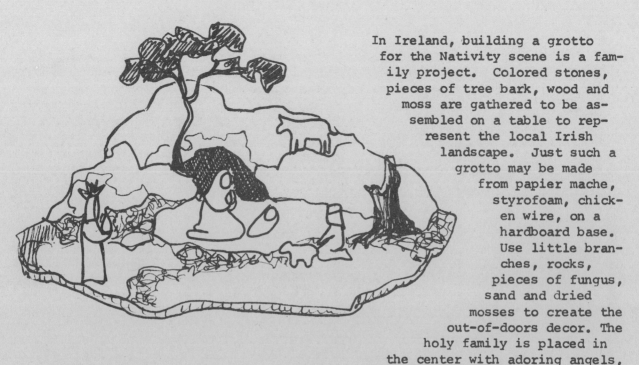

In Ireland, building a grotto for the Nativity scene is a family project. Colored stones, pieces of tree bark, wood and moss are gathered to be assembled on a table to represent the local Irish landscape. Just such a grotto may be made from papier mache, styrofoam, chicken wire, on a hardboard base. Use little branches, rocks, pieces of fungus, sand and dried mosses to create the out-of-doors decor. The holy family is placed in the center with adoring angels, animals, shepherds, and wise men nearby. The Irish custom is to move the wise men closer to the Christ child each day of the holy season.

To make the grotto, cut two sheets of styrofoam 1 and 2 inches thick in irregular land shapes. These should be large enough to accomodate the figures. Glue these to the hardboard, building different levels. Form the mountain with fine chicken wire and papier mache made with short strips of newsprint dipped in 1 part water, 1 part white glue. It is also good to have some made with finely chopped pieces of newsprint; soak in mixture and squeeze out when applying to wire. Continue applying papier mache until thick and rough and resembling a mountain with a small cave near where the holy family will be placed. Cover foam with thin layer of papier mache to give it the appearance of ground, paint it with white glue and cover with sand. Glue pieces of wood,

fungus, moss, and stones to edges of risers. Paint mountain with dark brown acrylic paint that may be obtained from any art store and sprinkle with sand, wood chips and stones at random, gluing with white glue where necessary. A green plant may be added to give a touch of life. The holy family may be made from a simple salt ceramic and painted with acrylic paints. Shapes need not be intricate. Simple forms of circles, balls, triangles and squares may be formed into human shapes. After initial shapes are made and dried, fabric dipped in white glue may be draped over figures for clothing and painted if desired.

The Ecuadorian "Pesebre" is made of a strong gift box 10"
x 7½" x 6½". To form door, cut three sides off cover of
box, leaving one long side. Tape long side of cover without edge to long side of box. Put a
triangle, 6" long and 3" high with
a 1" x 6" lip on base, from a
piece of cardboard. Glue
lip to top of box, triangle
forming peak of box. Paint
inside and outside of box
with thick paint made of
white latex with a little
sand mixed in for texture.
Paint designs with bright
colored paints.

Make figures from bak-
ers' clay. For hay un-
der Jesus, mold a 2" x
1½" x ½" oval; roll out
a 3½" circle ¼" thick
and press center of cir-
cle into center of oval;
with scissors cut one-
inch cuts all the way a-
round. Baby body is 2½"
oval with smaller oval for
head. Press body into hay.
Make small thin coils to trim face
and make crosses on body. Hands are two small balls of clay, and halo a
1½" circle 1/8" thick pressed onto back of head. Mary's body is 5" tall.
Form body from a simple shape with only arms and hands defined. Round
bottom front of figure to indicate knees. Attach hair ending just below
neck. To make cloak roll out an irregular 5½" x 7" x 1/8" piece of clay;
fold this around figure exposing upper part of body; press cloak to body.
Fold back top of cloak which is next to the head. Remaining figures are
molded in a similar manner. Joseph stands about 5" high and the lamb, a-
bout 2" high. Insert wire in angels back for hanging. After figures
are baked at 350° for 45 minutes, paint and spray with matt varnish.

The mission creche is constructed from a rectangular box,
cut-out arches, and two
cardboard pillars made
from scored cardboard
attached. Cut a styro-
foam ball in half and
glue to top of pillars.
The bell tower is made
of a piece of stiff
cardboard ½" the depth
of the top of the mis-
sion. It is then
scored and shaped like
picture. Tape the tow-
er to the top of the
mission and paint with
thick coats of latex
paint to which coffee
grounds have been add-
ed. Colors should be
tans or light brown. In-
side of mission should
be painted white.

Make a small bell by
covering a plastic pill
cup with either paper or fabric, then coat it with acrylic matt varnish.
Glue or wire to bell tower.

Make the little cross from fine wood strips that are lashed together.
Make a small slit in top of bell tower and insert bottom of cross
through bell tower ¼". Drop a generous amount of white glue around
base of cross and let dry. Decorate with designs in bright colors similar to picture.

Figures may be carved from soap or balsa wood and painted with acrylic
paint. Use very simple circular shapes. For animal shapes find simple
silhouettes in children's coloring books. Trace on either soap or wood
and carve.

This African creche is cut from the bottom
of a large oatmeal box. The opening is cut
out and a heavy construction paper cone
taped on for the roof. Glue or sew straw
to the roof allowing it to extend down in an
irregular pattern to look like picture. Paint
inside and out with thick coats of latex
paint, with sand mixed in it, to resemble
adobe.

Beautiful little African figures may be
purchased from SERRV, or you may make
your own from bakers' clay or carved
from balsa. Use simple shapes and
tint skin tones brown.

This little Far East creche can be made in any size you wish with boxes of different sizes, two cardboard tubes, and three styrofoam balls. For the main building find a box that has a lid. It should be about 4 inches deep. Cut a circular window in the top and a smaller circular window in the bottom so that they line up when lid is put on box. Paint inside of boxes with white latex paint, glue and tape box together. Add towers of cardboard tubes, topped with styrofoam balls and a dome of half a large styrofoam ball. Arrange flat boxes as in diagram and tape down to piece of heavy cardboard of hardboard. Coat all structures with a thick layer of latex paint to which sand has been added. Let it set a few minutes and texture more with a sponge. For trees, insert dried weeds in cardboard or anchor with florist's clay. Cover base with sand. Add figures to complete creche.

The "Ceppo" is the Italian version of the Christmas tree. It came into existence as a substitute for the burning of the Yule log and its shape represents the flames. The "Presepio" or nativity scene found in every Italian home is placed on the bottom shelf. These figures were often hand-carved--and there was often much competition to see who could create the most unusual ones. The next shelf above the crib held small gifts for children. These were placed there secretly by parents, relatives or friends. Candles that are fastened to the sides are always lighted on Christmas eve.

To construct: cut three 48" lengths of 3/4" square white pine. Taper ends to fit at top; glue and nail together to form pyramid. For shelves; cut four equilateral triangles measuring 23½", 16½", and 5½" from ½" plywood. Nail shelves and candle holders made from jar lids to framework; paint with red enamel. Glue red ball fringe to shelves.

To "hang-it-all" seems to be the thing these days. Here's our version of the hanging "Ceppo". It would be beautiful if done in monochromatic browns or greens.

You may make your own pattern for the three-section macrame sling or make the simple one we suggest here.

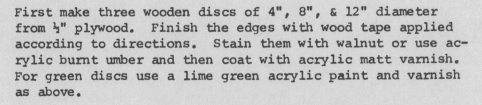

First make three wooden discs of 4", 8", & 12" diameter from ½" plywood. Finish the edges with wood tape applied according to directions. Stain them with walnut or use acrylic burnt umber and then coat with acrylic matt varnish. For green discs use a lime green acrylic paint and varnish as above.

To make the sling measure and cut six strands of heavy jute, 10', either light brown or dark green, depending on the color scheme you choose. If you can only find light weight jute, double the strands. At one end take all six strands and make a single knot. Measure down 6"; gather two adjoining strands and make another single knot. Repeat this procedure making 3-6" strands which are double. Now measure down 3" and take one strand and match it with one strand of the adjoining section (See diagram). Repeat with other two. Measure again 3" and knot all strands together as in the beginning.

Now measure down 10", repeating procedure of first section of sling. Then 5" and 5".

The next step is to repeat the procedure using the lengths 16", 8". After you tie the last total knot, leave a tassel of at least 6".

Insert wooden circles in slings. To make them level when they hang, use a little white glue to secure jute to wood so they won't slip. A possible arrangement for your hanging "Ceppo" would be a standing star on the top shelf (See diagram), three angels on the second sheld, and the holy family on the bottom and largest shelf. Use any of the suggested ideas to create your own figures if you wish.

A contemporary setting for the creche might be a large Christmas
ball that hangs from the ceiling, like a hanging light fixture. It
can be made by inflating a large heavy balloon such as a weather balloon or one of those heavy ones that children have to bounce on. In-
flate and coat the balloon with strips of newsprint dipped in a solution of 1 part water, 1 part white glue, 1 part wallpaper paste. Put
about 4 thicknesses over all the balloon. Let dry. Draw with marker where the opening will be on the dried newsprint. Now cover all
of balloon except the area that is to be the opening with prepared
papier mache or make you own with finely chopped newsprint and the a-
bove solution. This mixture has a rather lumpy texture and should be
applied at least ¼" thick. Let dry. Let air
out of balloon and carefully snip original
coat of papier mache around marked opening and take the balloon out. Paint
with white latex paint inside and out.
Drill small holes in the top and a-
round opening to weave fine wire for
holding tiny white lights and also
for attaching the ring and chain
for hanging. An old lamp swag
works very well, and an extension
cord plug may be connected to wir-
ing just inside top of the balloon.
Insert where the balloon tie off
had been. Using fine wire attach ring and swag chain to ball.
Wire small string of tiny white
lights to the inside of opening and
plug into receptacle at top, fastening again with wire. Touch up all exposed
pieces of wire on outside of ball with white
latex paint. Insert a circular piece of cardboard that will fit just below opening for a sturdy place for figures. Tape into place and touch up
with paint. Cut the bottom 1/3 of a circular salt box off and cover with
gold paper and trims. Slit top and slip down over chain and ring next to
ball. Glue fast with white glue. Add a trim of gold tinsel rope around o-
pening with white glue and your own imagination on placing figures, making
a unique creche. Straw or angels; hair may be fastened to background for
atmosphere. If using straw, be sure to keep it away from lights. Gluing
it down with white glue will help.

163

We've made the creche in shapes of
missions, huts, and grottoes, so
why not an American hip-roofed
barn with corn husk figures
and little clay animals and
a loft full of straw?

Our barn is made from a
12" shoe box. Cut 2/3
of the bottom, length-
wise as in picture.
The remaining 1/3 will
be the stable fence
behind our figures.
Cut a piece of heavy
cardboard 16" x 4".
Score making 4-4" sec-
tions. Shape like hip-
roof and tape to shoe
box. Glue wood shingles
to roof with white glue.
Make top section overlap
just a bit and make eaves
of about ½" as in picture.

Paint fence design and inside of barn with brown latex paint, including loft.
Paint outside of barn with red acrylic paint and trim with white.

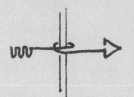

Glue a very thin slat of wood in the middle of the back
from stable floor to crown of roof. Shape to roof and
trim. Paint brown. For weathervane, use a 3" piece of
no. 9 wire and make arrow from a softer finer wire. Wrap
and fasten with a drop of glue to hold (See diagram.)

Make two 1" diameter stars from construction paper, glue together over
wire, and coat with acrylic matt varnish. Drill a little hole in point of
roof and insert weathervane, secure with a drop of white glue. Put straw
in the mow. Make two little doves from construction paper and hang from
barn roof by thread tied to straight pin and inserted in cardboard.

To make corn husk dolls: Soak corn husks in a
solution of 1 tbs. bleach to 2 c. water for a
few hours or over night. This will soften and
bleach the husks. For head and body of Mary, cut
a piece of husk in a 10" length. Make a small
ball of cotton or lint from the dryer. Fold
over damp corn husk and shape around ball for
head--tie with natural colored thread. Add a

164

larger roll of cotton or lint for body. Before
tying waist, make arms by rolling a pipe cleaner
with husk in a 4" length; tie at both ends to
make hands. Insert this in back of doll, put cotton
on top, and shape husk around. Tie off waist (see
diagram.)

For Mary, add another skirt of husk, and tie off at waist. Add a husk shawl
over her head that comes about to her waist. Glue in place. Cut a little
fan from husk and glue to back of head for halo. For baby, make just a two-
section body, with head the smaller of the sections. Glue a little husk
shawl around body, and add halo. Joseph is made in much the same manner
except that the legs are made like the arms, only much thicker and are tied
in when waist is tied. A little flat brim black hat made of construction
paper adds much. Hair, eyes, and mouth may be drawn on with fine point
pen or paint. Other creche figures may be made in much the same manner.
Experiment with making animals also; or make them from clay, soap, or wood.

An easy to assemble, but very effective way, to make creche figures
is as follows: The bodies are cut from an 8" circle and the arms
from a 4" circle. If you want larger figures adjust according-
ly. Use one quarter of the larger circle for the body and
one quarter of the smaller circle for each arm. Cut from
heavy art or construction paper. Pin to desired fabric and
cut 1/2" all around and glue over paper. Twist into cone
shapes, glue in place. Attach arms to body cone 1/4" from
point. Plastic ball heads are covered with nylon taped to
inside of the cone. Glue on desired trims to bodies using your own imagination.

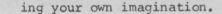

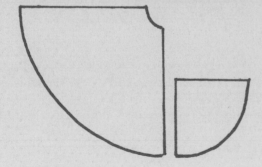

165

Advent Wreaths
may be made of --

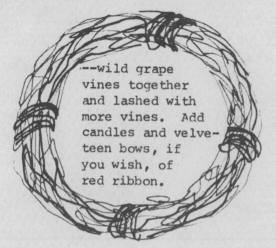

--wild grape vines together and lashed with more vines. Add candles and velveteen bows, if you wish, of red ribbon.

---- branches of pine, cedar or spruce. Form a clothes hanger in the shape of a circle -- using fine wire. Wrap small pieces of evergreen around and around until a thick and even wreath is formed. Add candle holders and ribbons, if desired.

---- straw wound with red ribbon. Add red candles.

---- pine cones and nuts. Drill and glue 2 inch wires in cones and nuts. Stick into straw or styrofoam wreath. Spray with matt varnish. Add candle holders.

 ---- milk weed pods, acorn caps and horse chestnuts that are wired and inserted in a straw wreath. Add ribbons and candles.

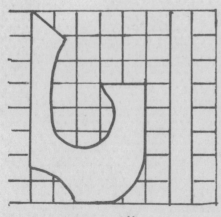

1 sq. = 1"

This wooden Advent candle holder is made from 1" pine boards, 5" wide. The center post is a 1" square piece. The four side pieces are glued securely to center post. Drill 5/8" holes for candles to be seated in. May be finished with stain and varnish or painted white.

166

Make a Della Robbia Advent wreath.
Begin with branches of pine
wired to a frame. Make little
marzipan-type fruits and vegetables from bakers' clay. Tint
with food coloring to look like
real fruit. Insert 2 inch wire,
bake as directed, and insert in
wreath. Spray the entire wreath
with acrylic matt varnish.

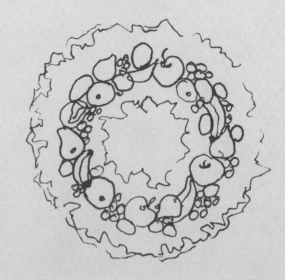

Bake upside down

To make candle holders to be inserted in wreaths, form a ball of
bakers' clay about 1½" in diameter.
Dip candle in flour and then into
clay. Form around candle base
leaving a rather heavy bottom. Insert piece of no. 9 wire 1½" long in
bottom (see diagram). Bake according to directions. Paint or decorate as you wish.

The rose is a symbol for
Christ. A beautiful wreath
may be made of simple paper
roses to be used for Advent.
Cut tissue paper in 30 inch by
5 inch strips. Fold to 2½"
strips. Roll to make flowers.
Wire ends, attach to plastic
foam ring. Leaves of construction paper painted with acrylic matt
varnish may be attached to wires and added.

*See section on Germany for
instructions on how to make
a German Advent Wreath stand.*

Candles candles candles

Candles can be made with frozen
juice cans or pringle cans as molds:
take an ice pick and make a hole in the
bottom center of can. Make hole large e-
nough to be able to pull candle wick through.

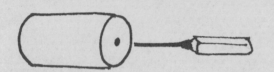

Pull wick through and tape with
masking tape or seal with floral
clay. Set mold in a container of
wet sand.

Wrap top of wick around pencil as in diagram--

Heat wax to about 190° in a metal bucket, pitcher,
or coffee can. Add stearing crystals to make a
harder wax. Pour wax into mold to ½" from top,
let cool, and fill cavity formed by cooling wax.

If you wish a 3 color effect, prepare mold as above, tilt
mold at an angle in sand like diagram. Pour in 1 color of
wax. Let wax cool till hard. Tilt mold the other direction
and pour in next color, cool till hard, etc. until you have all
the colors you wish. Then stand mold
straight and add last layer.

Candles can also be made
from jello molds, milk cartons,
in glass cups and glasses (leave
them in the mold-drill hole and insert wick).
Float little ones in water-hang big ones in slings.

For frosted candles, prepare mold as above, and pour white wax in mold. Set
in cold water until ¼" of wax hardens around sides of mold. Insert ice pick
to carefully remove any air bubbles that might form. Pour wax out of center back into heating pan. Chill until very cold (mold). Heat a dark
color of wax to 180° and pour into chilled cavity. Set in cold water
until all wax is hard.

Snow candles: Bring in large deep dishpan
full of snow. Make a cavity in the snow
with your hand, not packing the snow too much.
Heat was to 180º and pour into snow. Let harden
and drill hole in wax for wick and insert it.
Experiment with different shapes that you can mold
in the snow with your hands. Also objects like pieces
of wood or metal may be imbedded in the snow and the
wax poured around them for unusual candles.

*Sand candles may
be cast in the same
manner, using
damp sand in a large
pan or box.*

The juice-can candles may be used in wide-mouth
quart salad dressing jars to give the look of a
hurricane lamp. These may be nestled in greens
without the danger of fire. Use a little gold
braid or tinsel rope around the top of the jar
to cover edge of the jar. Pringle-can candles
may be inserted in gallon jars and hung in macrame slings.

169

Puppet People

by Galene J. Myers

The Bible is an endless source of characters and plots suitable for puppet plays, skits, and episodes. Puppetry portrays the religious and the supernatural with more impact than live drama, for it transcends human limitations and presents tragedy convincingly. Yes, the limp and lifeless puppets you have made come alive on the magic stage, truly puppet people.

There are three types of puppets: hand or glove puppets, stringed marionettes, and silhouettes or shadow puppets. Bible characters and costumes can be readily adapted to each type, but since hand puppets and marionettes resemble real people, they are more commonly used. A new trend of "stick" puppets, similar to the old shadow puppets, may be adapted to the younger set.

Hand puppets and marionettes are similar, in that the head must be the principal part. In the hand puppet head, the neck is hollow to control movement and to support the garments in contrast to the solid neck of the marionette, from which the body parts are hung. Ancient puppet heads were carved from wood.

Today puppet heads are made from the wood fiber in cardboard and paper, from sawdust paste, and plastic wood. These heads are light enough to be manipulated on hand puppets, and can be heavy enough to balance a marionette properly. The "stick" puppets are made of heavy cardboard with faces or figures mounted on them.

The neck of the hand puppet is a simple cardboard tube, made to fit the forefinger of the puppeteer. A piece of flexible cardboard 3" x 3½" is about right for an adult hand, if you wish to insert the tube in a stuffed cloth head, a styrofoam egg, or use papier-mache or sawdust paste.

A 4½" length of the cardboard tube used to make rolls of commercial paper may be cut to make a neck tube and the semblance of a head at the other end, which may be used as is, or modeled with paste to make a more durable head. See Figures 1,2,3.

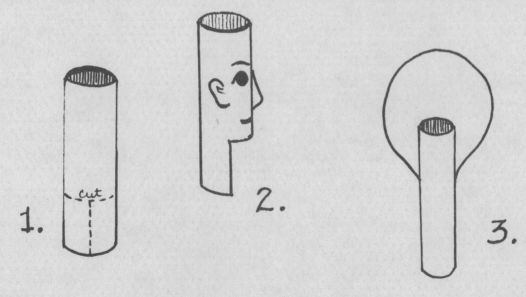

1.   2.   3.

Miniature marionettes may be made with bits of wood, fastened together with cloth joints, dressed, and strung together with five strings from an infant control of cardboard. In a 6-8" marionette, use a small oval face of wood, with the main control string tied to a screw eye in the top of the head, one string on each hand, one from each foot. Pull the strings through holes in the cardboard, and tie to a button larger than the hole. Fasten the head string first; and, with the marionette feet flat on the floor, tie the hand strings first, next the feet. The marionette can perform by a slight turn of the control.

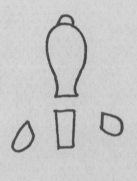

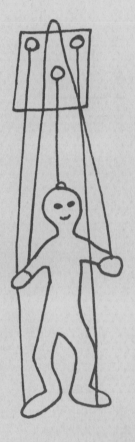

Miniature Marionettes

6 - 8" high

Variation in stringing. Use a continuous string from hand to hand, threading through the hole, tied to a button.

A string from the middle of the back to the control, will make the puppet bow.

Puppets to "stick-up" from behind a curtain are simple oval, flat face, made on heavy cardboard with a neck handle.
It is better to paint the faces and add hair for a realistic performance. Punch a hole in the neck to hang the puppet.

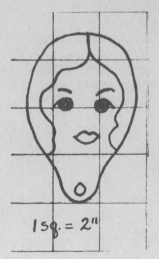

1 sq. = 2"

"Stick-up" puppet, made from heavy cardboard.

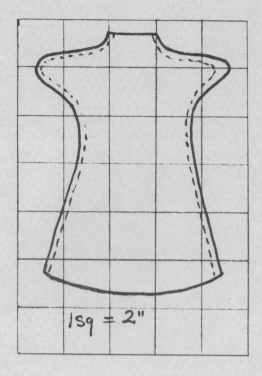

1 sq = 2"

Hand puppet garment, cut 2
pieces, seam on dotted lines.
Use plain unbleached muslin.
The pattern is for mitten
hands. If other hands are
to be used, leave opening
and insert form.

Although more commercial puppets are
now available, puppetry remains a challenge to individual creativity. Make
them from household discards and inexpensive materials such as styrofoam, sponge
rubber, and remnants. Create your own
puppets, and start a repertoire of dramas,
plays, poems, songs and music. Arrange
curtains to hide the puppeteers, add a
small cassette for recording and playing
back, and you are off to the "magic stage"
of puppetry. Good puppetry will use all
your creative genius and cultivate more.

Such as playwriting! If you are interested in Bible history, remember that
the Bible itself is an almost undiscovered source of play material, the history of music and song writers is another, and your home town history.

PATTERN FOR A PLAY

A puppet play portrays episodes from life by means of dialogue, in one or
more acts. It can be combined with robed live choirs and turned into a mag-
ical fairyland with lighting and music. Look first for a magnificent character, an unusual story. Live with it, and the play will almost write itself.

MODELING PASTE

Commercial wall paper paste makes an excellent paste for papier-mache. Mixed
with sawdust it provides a modeling paste for making heads. Mix the sawdust
with the powder and add the water slowly in order to have a firm, putty-like
paste, which can be easily shaped and modeled. Keep in a covered container.

When modeling on the neck tube, cover the end with gummed paper tape. Place
a small quantity of paste firmly over the end and dry. This will give a good
base to finish the head. Use water to smooth and shape.

The sawdust paste can also be used for making props, or the thinned paste, to
model items such as instruments with papier-mache. The puppet heads when
thoroughly dry should be covered with a thin coating of papier-mache, from one
or two layers of paper toweling. Dry before painting.

The trees of Christmas

The Christmas tree had its origin in early Christian homes in Germany and Scandinavia. In fact the worship of trees goes far back into the ancient history of Scandinavia. This custom was adapted to become part of their Christmas festivals when they became Christian.

One legend from Germany tells how an English missionary named Winfrid (later known as Boniface) while traveling through northern Germany encountered a group of people preparing to sacrifice little Prince Asulf to the god Thor. Winfrid stopped the sacrifice and cut down "the blood oak." As the oak fell, a young fir tree appeared. Winfrid told the people that the fir was the tree of life, representing Christ. The custom of decorating a tree was then to become a symbol for German Christians celebrating the birth of Christ. They decorated it with stars, angels, toys, gilded nuts, and candies wrapped in bright papers. Later they added tinsel and lighted candles. The Scandinavians originally trimmed their trees with fish nets and little flags. Now they also use Christmas cookies, apples, and gilded nuts. People in Poland decorate with bright paper ornaments and candles.

Christmas trees need not always be discarded after Christmas. Why not purchase a live tree that is balled and burlapped for planting? Be sure to place it in the coolest part of the room--away from heat. Place in a large container, spray the tree with wilt-proofing latex before trimming, and keep the soil moist. After Christmas set the tree in a cooler place until such time as you can plant it. Be sure to keep the soil moist until planting time.

Decorate your tree with things you make --

Stuffed gingham or patchwork stars, hearts, birds,
and angels   (Early American)
Ornaments of straw   (Sweden, Norway, Denmark)

Braided little baskets filled with candy (Poland, Germany)

Cookies (Sweden, Germany)

Icons made from bakers clay (Greece)

Paper birds and nests (Mexico)

Bread dough ornaments (Ecuador)

Lacy stars made from paper doilies (American)

Felt, milk weed pods, seeds, popcorn, egg cartons, corn husks and
foil. (More detailed information on how to make the above
are included on the pages to follow.)

Handcrafted Decorations

Angels made of corn husks.

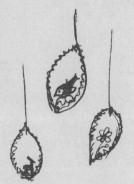

Snowflakes made from paper doilies. Staple every other circle on outside edge of doily forming a three-dimensional decoration. Punch out center circle and hang by tiny wire or regular Christmas tree hanger.

Dried milk weed pods that have been sprayed with gold or silver. Decorate with trims from sewing basket around the edge and little dried flowers, weeds or tiny plastic birds glued into place. Add wire hangers.

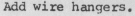

Decorations made from cookie dough and clear candies to look like stained glass windows. Use a stiff cookie dough similar to the Lucia ginger snaps.
        Make long rolls of dough and form outline of cookie and interior lines-design on cookie sheet and bake according to directions. Take out of oven and add broken pieces of clear candies in sections--return to oven and heat just until candies melt. Remove from oven and cool. It is best to use a teflon cookie sheet.

Decorations cont'd

Styrofoam or papier-mache balls with
dried seeds such as peas, beans of all
kinds. Glue on with white glue in desired patterns. Coat outside with melted
paraffin to give a frosted look. Add a
wire hanger.

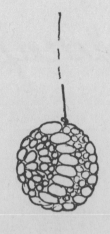

Mexican braids: Braid three colors of tissue
paper into long braids--form into circles within
circles, circle chains, little baskets for hold-
ing candy, or any variation you might wish.

For an old fashioned decoration, make little popcorn balls with yarn hangers. If you wish to eat
them on Christmas, wrap each ball in a square
of clear plastic wrap and tie with ribbon or yarn
for hanging.

POPCORN BALLS

5 qts. popped corn--keep hot in 300° oven.
In buttered heavy pan combine:
        2 c. sugar
        1½ c. water
        ½ tsp. salt
        ¼ c. lt. corn syrup
        1 tsp. vinegar

Cook to hard ball stage (250°). Stir
in 1 tsp. vanilla. Slowly pour over
popcorn, stirring just to mix. Butter
hands and form balls.

175

Pieces of felt, rickrack and/or trims, quilted
with a sewing machine around patterns and
tied with a yarn loop to hang on the tree.

Greek icons made from bakers clay rolled thin and patterns put on with little rolls of clay. Bake according to directions and paint with acrylic paints. Spray
with acrylic spray.

Stuffed gingham or patchwork decorations are made
with two pieces of fabric sewn together leaving a
2½" opening for turning and stuffing slightly
with old nylons or cotton or polyester batting.
Add trims, etc. Use your own creativity in
creating patterns and trims.

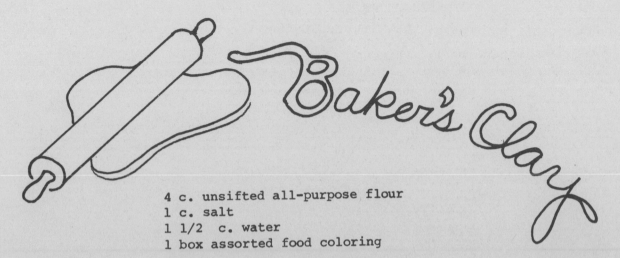

Baker's Clay

4 c. unsifted all-purpose flour
1 c. salt
1 1/2 c. water
1 box assorted food coloring

(More brilliant colors may be obtained from
a bakery supply store.)

Mix flour and salt in a bowl. Stir in water until mixture can
be pressed into a ball. Turn out onto floured board or pastry
cloth and knead until smooth. Clay should be the consistency that
is easy to handle so that it can be rolled and molded without
flaking apart or sticking to hands. If necessary, use extra flour
or water sparingly for proper consistency. Yield: 2 1/2 lbs. clay.

Make patterns for symbols actual size on paper and
use as a guide while shaping dough directly on an
ungreased baking sheet. Color small amounts of clay
as you need it. Colors remain same during baking.
Pack pieces together tightly as you would in handling
real ceramic clay. Insert paper clip in top for
hanging.

When using coloring in dough, bake at 200° F.
for 40 to 50 minutes and turn, baking 40 to 50
more minutes. For uncolored ceramic figures,
bake at 375° F. for 35 to 40 minutes or longer
until completely dried out.

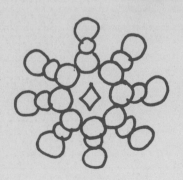

Egg carton ornaments

Egg cartons of papier-mache, cut into sections points, and glued together. Paint with white latex paint and trim with rickrack or other trims to make little baskets for tiny sprays of wild dried flowers or weeds, little plastic animals or Nativity figures, or candy to hang on a tree.

Tissue paper fruit

MATERIALS: Colored tissue paper, stapler, white glue, light weight cardboard for pattern, and string to hang ornaments.

Cut pattern of each fruit from cardboard. Use these patterns to cut ornaments from layered sheets of tissue paper. 16 layers for apple and orange, 14 for pear, 13 for lemon, peach and plum, 10 for leaf. Draw line down center of tissue as noted in pattern. Staple layered sheets of tissue vertically on this line. Using toothpick dipped in white glue, fasten tissue together as in diagram, joining points marked 1 together, then points marked 3. Press together gently at edges to secure. On next sheet glue point 2 to point 2 of first sheet and point 4 the same fashion. The next sheet fasten points 1 and 3 as you began. Continue until tissue is all glued and ornament is completed. Leaves are made just like the fruit except the last 2 sheets are not glued together so that leaf will not be completely round. For stems, roll up 1" square of black paper and glue to top of fruit. For orange, glue a tiny black star to bottom and a leaf to the top. Make loops for hanging with needle and thread.

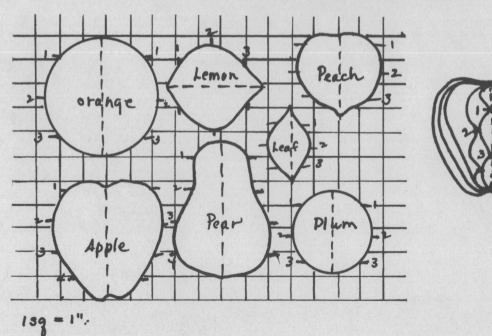

1 sq = 1".

178

Paper ornaments

Cut a square of white shiny paper
any size you wish. Fold in half and
then in half again.

Then fold diagonally, making a triangular
piece.

Make cuts from sides
in similar fashion to
diagram or make up your
own.

Open, and refold in and out to make a dimensional design. You may
cut designs as intricately as you wish.

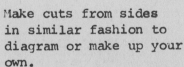

Danish paper baskets

Make two strips of
paper 2" side and 6"
long. One white and
one colored. Fold in
half. (1)

Draw light line 3/4" from cut edge and make a semi-circle. Cut.
Cut two slits from folded edge to line. (2)

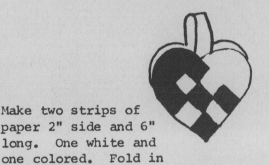

Place two folded halves of heart side by side
with curved edges down. (3)

To weave, start with bottom loop of
white half. Insert white loop into
first colored loop. Now open white
loop and insert second colored loop,
and so on to end of row. (4)

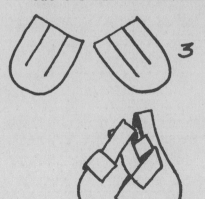

For the second row, take middle loop, insert
first colored loop in middle white loop, then
open middle colored loop and insert middle white
in it. Open white loop and insert next colored
loop in it.

Weave third row in the same manner as second row, taking care not to tear
the paper in this last row. Attach 1" by 6" strip of paper for handle, or
use scraps of ribbon or colored string.

Swedish paper birds

These paper birds may be used for decorations or with
a little printed note inside could be used for Christmas
cards. Make them from a stiff paper such as construction
paper, 8 1/2" by 11". Fold in half and cut on heavy lines.

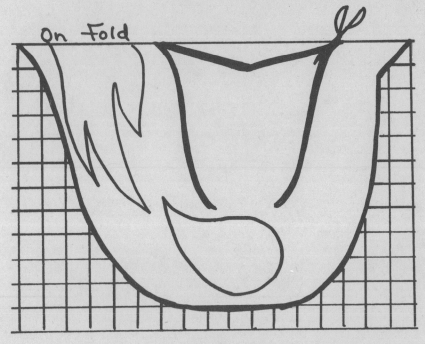

On Fold

Fold feet to the inside
and fasten with a staple
or tape. Make wings and
tail feathers from a con-
trasting color. Glue in
place.

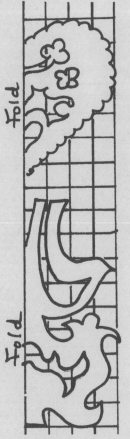

Fold

Fold

Cards and notes can be made of cut paper silhouettes
similar to those pictured here. Fold a piece of paper
in half and cut designs. Open and glue to a contrasting
color of paper. Use your creativity to make new
designs of your own.

To make a perfect 5 pointed star

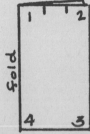

A Fold square of paper once down center; mark corners 1-2-3-4 as shown, on both sides. Mark top 1-2 into thirds.

Fold corner 4 down to mark at left of 2; mark new corners 5 and 6.

B

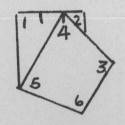

Starting at 5, bring 6 up toward 4 so that folded edges are flush. Mark new corner 7.

C

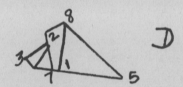

D

Turn entire piece over so that corner 3 is at left instead of at right. Fold 1-5 back flush with 5-7; mark new corner 8.

Mark edge 1-5 in half, cutting from ¼" below corner 8 to this mark (broken line) will produce a conventional flat star. For a star with a 3-dimensional effect, mark top half of edge 1-5 in half again; cut from same starting point to this mark.(see solid line). Arrange long folds out, short folds in.

E

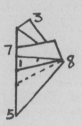

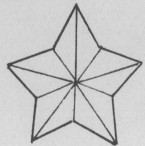

Gifts you make

Make a patchwork cracker basket.
Early pioneer women used these baskets
extensively because of a lack of dishes
and baskets.

Sew 4 pieces to bottom, then sew
up sides. Make lining of same
dimensions. Insert lining,
turn in top edges and top stitch.
Make handle of patches put together
in a 12" x 6" piece.
Fold and sew. Turn right side out. Stitch
under ends and top stitch to basket. Cardboard
base may be added, but this would limit washing.

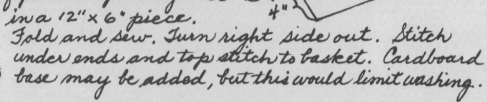

5" by 8"

4"

Patchwork shopping bags, lined with plain cotton
fabric also make an interesting and useful gift.
They fold up into a small package for carrying in
purse until needed.

Patch piece 14" by 24". Sew up bottom and side after folding
in half to make a piece 12" by 14". Make lining the same way.
Insert lining. Fold in at top to make finished edge and top
stitch. Make handle similar to cracker basket handle.

Finger puppets made from pieces of felt or double knit,
sewn around outside edge make a delightful gift
for children. Eyes and mouth, hair, etc.
may be made of felt and yarn, glue or sew
on.

Crazy crunch sewing baskets: Using empty plastic
containers such as large Cool Whip containers,
commercial 5lb. cottage cheese containers. Make
a patchwork piece or just a piece of cotton fabric.
in a bright colored pattern, the size of the lid.
Make a little pin cushion of the same or contrasting
fabric and sew to base piece. Sew on loops or trims
to hold scissors, tape measure, and thimble. Glue
to lid. Add the above. The box may be filled with
crazy crunch below. Add a yarn bow and it need
not be wrapped.

CRAZY CRUNCH:

4 qt. popped popcorn
1 1/3 c. pecans
2/3 c. almonds

Combine and boil over medium heat for
10-15 minutes   1 c. Margarine
                     1 1/3 c. sugar
                     1 tsp. vanilla
                     1 c. clear corn syrup

Pour hot mixture over popcorn and spread
on cookie sheet to dry. Break up into
small pieces. Keeps well.

A gift of something living is a special kind
of gift for everyone. Flower pots may be covered
with yarn glued on in Mexican deco-style; fabric
covers may be glued to pot, patch work style;
velveteen ribbon or fabric may be used; fringes
of different kinds may be glued to cool whip
containers to set pots in; little baskets may
be made or bought to set pots in. Almost any
container such as an old fashioned tea kettle,
cup, or vase can make an interesting planter.
Pots may also be hung in slings made of rug
yarn or jute, using simple knots.

Make a riding toy for a tiny tot by making
a stuffed top such as our turtle, glue and
take to a piece of 3/8" plywood and screw on
an old roller skate to the bottom. The larger
the toy the more roller skates needed.

1 sq.= 1½"

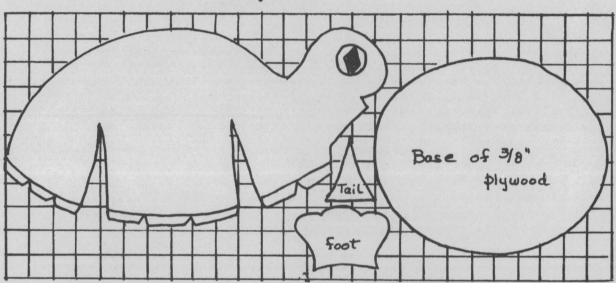

Tail

Foot

Base of 3/8"
plywood

Sew back seam and darts, stuff with old nylons, or cotton or polyester batting. Feet and tail are made of felt. Tack fabric around and to underside
of board. Glue feet and tail to board so that they stick out from under
board. Glue on eyes made of felt. Lines on turtle may be made with liquid
embroidery or embroidered on with yarn before stuffing.

POMANDER APPLES: you will need 2 boxes of
whole cloves for each apple. Beginning at
top of apple, insert cloves as close as possible all over apple. Place in warm dry
place (preferably in the sun) for about one
week. Make a tassel of bright red yarn.
For friends, a sweet scented gift that will
last and last.

184

Empty jars and cans make clever banks
and storage for tiny things such as
fish hooks, matches and odds and ends.
Glue on felt or spray paint and
decorate with trims from the sewing
basket.

Zig-Zag a patchwork table cloth together-

TRIVETS may be made of heavy twine, string, yarn
or rope coiled and glued to a cardboard base with
white glue. You may dye the cord a desired color.
Paint the cardboard base with latex paint before
gluing cord in place. Press trivet under heavy
books overnight so they will dry flat.

A casserole carrier can be made much the same
manner as the trivet. Turn casserole upside
down and cover as smoothly as possible with
plastic wrap. Tape edges with masking tape
to the inside of the dish. Soak clothesline
in a solution of half glue and half liquid
starch. Start at middle of bottom and wind
in spiral fashion to cover bottom. Cut pieces
of rope and make spirals and loops for sides.
Spiral a second mat over the first one. Dry
thoroughly. Remove from casserole and dry
off casserole before painting.

Fanciful home made FIRE STICKS for lighting
the fireplace can be made by rolling a
large sheet of newspaper diagonally and
tightly. Glue to secure. Drip candle
wax on end of paper roll to insure flama-
bility. Now roll a piece of brightly
colored paper tightly around newspaper
and glue to secure.

Create a container from a tall fruit juice can or oatmeal box. Cover with
pieces of colored paper, wrap with bright colored yarn, collage with wrinkled
foil, or wrap with jute or binder twine.

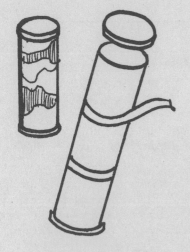

A very unusual gift for the bathroom is a tissue
container made from three 2 lb. coffee cans.
Remove all the ends except the bottom of one can.
Be sure to save two of the plastic lids that fit
the cans. Using masking tape, fasten three cans
together as diagram. Cover can with bright colored fabric, felt, fake fur, or patchwork pieces.
Use white glue to adhere covering to can. Put
one plastic lid on the bottom to protect the floor
from rust stain and use other lid for a cover.
Will hold 4 rolls of tissue.

Mildred Heckert suggests the pattern and idea for using old Christmas cards
to make a little basket for new cards or candies. Use two cards back to
back for bottom and sides. Stitch together with blanket stitch using yarn.
First join sides to bottom, then whip up sides. If desired, punch holes
at the top of sections and tie red ribbon bows at the six corners.

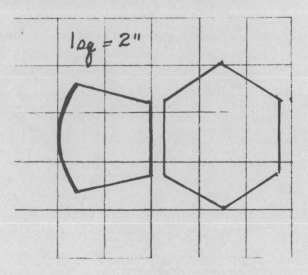

1 sq = 2"

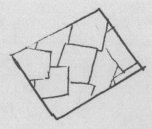

Another idea for use of Christmas cards is to
make placemats for the holidays by using floral
paper mats, collage back side with old greeting cards, cover both sides with clear contact
paper.

186

Mittens Mittens

A mitten tree would make an interesting Christmas project that would provide special gifts for needy families in cold climates. Mittens may be crocheted knit or made from fabrics.

A new pattern from a very old idea for making mittens has been designed by Esther Rupel, associate professor of clothing and textiles at Purdue University. Enclosed is a diagram for a small mitten. To obtain complete instructions and pattern in six sizes, write for the Cooperative Extension Bulletin HE 536 "Mittens, Mittens, Mittens." Mailing Room, AGAD Building, Purdue University, West Lafayette, Indiana, 47907. Enclose 40¢ to cover cost and handling charges. A companion bulletin, HE 538 "How to Make Helmet Hoods" is available. Both may be purchased for 75¢.

Mittens may be made from new or recycled sturdy fabric: corduroy, wool, or heavy double knit, and lined with lighter weight fabric. Pin the three pattern pieces on a double layer of fabric, and cut. Line the pieces individually before assembling mitten. First stitch the cuff edge, right sides together. Turn and understitch to avoid pressing. Stitch twice across the back for a casing. Insert elastic and secure ends with stitching. Join finger and palm sections to form the thumb. Clip seam and join to back. Turn mitten right side out. Now make the second mitten to complete the pair.

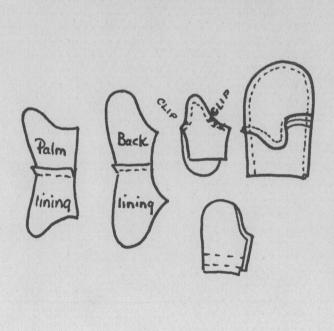

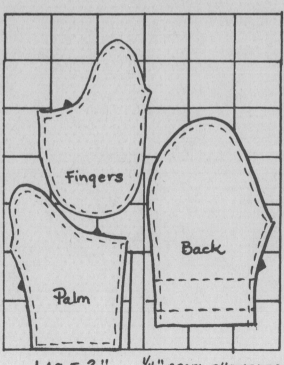

1 sq = 2"   ¼" seam allowance

wrapagift

Gift wraps may be made from white shelf
paper and decorated in a variety of ways.

For a splatter effect, cut a piece of shelf paper 20"
by 24". Fold in half, open, and drip poster paint
thinned with a few drops of water along crease--fold
paper over and smooth gently with hand--open and dry. Add
second color same manner--open and dry. Add color until you have
desired effect.

Use a roller dipped in colored paint. Make a pattern with it on the paper.
Press and pull string. Open and dry.

Cut an onion, a small cabbage, or a lemon, dip in color, print. Or cut a
potato in patterns and dip in paint and print.

Dip edges of paper towels in dye, let dry. Towels may also be folded
in different ways and corners dipped in dye--open and let dry.

Tie-dye old sheets. Press and use for wrapping
packages.

Use the want ad sections of
Sunday papers as a gift wrap.
Tie with bright colored
yarns.

Drop wet ink or thin paint
on shelf paper and blow
with a straw to make
unusual patterns.

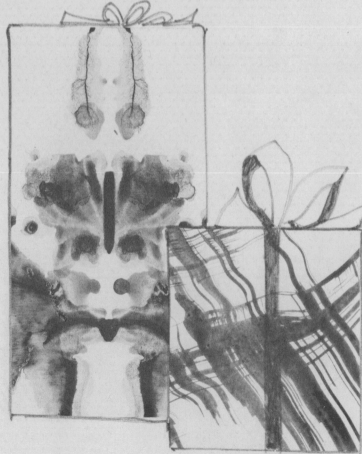

Silk screen cards

A delightful and inexpensive way to make Christmas
cards is the art of silk screen. Silk screen is
a print making technique used
by artists and can be as simple
or as intricate as you wish.
The process we use is com-
prised of simple materials
found in your kitchen, the
nearest Five-and-Dime and
supermarket.

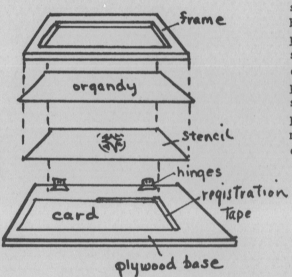

MATERIALS: 1/3 yd. cotton organdy, a
simple wooden frame contructed from 1"
by 1" pine or an old 8" by 10" wooden
picture frame; a piece of ½" plywood
slightly larger than the frame, white glue,
cornstarch, detergent, unflavored gelatin,
powdered dye or Skript ink, an 8" size
squeegee, heavy tracing paper, heavy bond
paper or 28# mimeo paper, masking tape,
measuring spoons, cups, scissors and plastic
containers with lids.

THE FRAME: Cut the organdy ½"
larger than the frame. Fasten it
to the frame on one side with tacks
or a wood stapler, stretching tightly.
Tack to opposite side of the frame,
making sure that the grain of the
fabric is straight as possible.
Finish tacking sides, again stretching as tightly as possible. Run a
bead of glue all around the frame where fabric meets the frame. Press with
your finger to make sure it saturates the fabric and adheres to the wood.
Let dry.

Center the screen on the
piece of plywood with
organdy side down. (see
diagram). Use two small
hinges to fasten the frame
to the plywood on one 8"
side.

STENCIL: Make the stencil
from heavy stencil paper.
You may use several of the
designs here or make your
own. One patter is created
for a card to fit a legal
size envelope, the other a
regular 3½" by 6½" envelope.
Enlarge the card pattern on
light weight paper and cut
out. Trace this pattern on
the heavier stencil paper
and cut with cuticle scissors.
Fasten the stencil to the
organdy with masking tape
(see diagram).

189

INK: Mix together 3/4 tsp. Rit dye in ½ c. boiling water *or* mix 4 tbs. of hot water with a 2 oz. bottle of Skript ink. In top of double boiler, stir together 2 tbs. cold water, 2 tbs. cornstarch and the color mix. Cook slowly until very thick. Remove from heat. Add dissolved gelatin. Cool. Store in plastic containers until ready to use. Refrigerate for long time storage. Bring to room temperature for use.

TO PRINT: Use a practice card. Place it in the registration guides. Lower screen and spoon a liberal amount of ink across the top of the screen. Draw the squeegee across the screen twice from top to bottom. Lift the screen and carefully remove the card. (The ink causes the card to adhere to the screen as it prints.) Print a second test card.

Then print as many cards as you wish. Set aside to dry.

Clean the screen after using by pulling off the stencil and scrub the screen with a soft brush under cold running water.

If you wish to make designs using more than one color, you may attach the second stencil to the organdy and print with the different color. I prefer to have more than one frame prepared so that there can be a frame for each color.

Fold cards in half and print your own message inside.

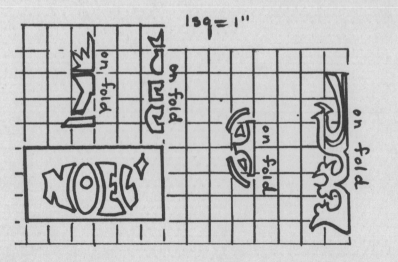

1 sq = 1"

Stencil Patterns

Wood cuts for Christmas cards:

materials:

1 set of inexpensive wood carving knives. They may be obtained from an import
shop or art supply store.
A piece of pine--1" by 3" by 5" for card to fit a regular size envelope
          1" by 3" by 8" for legal size envelope

          Make sure wood has no knots and is not heavily grained unless
          you wish to use those lines as part of your design.

1 brayer--may be obtained from an art supply store
Water base block printing ink, your choice of color
A cookie sheet
A wooden spoon
A good 28# paper or rice paper

instructions:

Make a simple pattern. Remember that all designs will be reversed when they
are printed. Do design on the wood with a fine point marker or flair pen. Cut
away areas you do not wish to have printed.

Put about 3 tbs. of ink on the cookie sheet. Roll brayer over the ink until the
brayer is completely covered with ink. Roll the brayer over the block that has
been carved. Press paper evenly on the inked block, leaving an even margin
around the block. Rub back of paper with the wooden spoon until all the paper
is inked and you can determine the pattern by the raised marks. Pull off paper
and let dry.

A second color may be added by preparing another block cut in a consistent
pattern to the first one.

You may also wish to make a patten, which is a board with guidelines for your
block to make printing easier and registration more perfect. For this, you will
need a piece of 1/4" hardboard, 8" by 10"; 2 pieces of 1" lumber, one 7" in
length and one 10" in length. Glue and nail them to the hardboard similar to
the diagram.

When printing, put block tightly in corner
and mark the registration (margins) with
masking tape on the 1" frame.

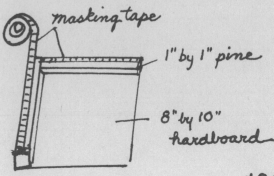

masking tape

1" by 1" pine

8" by 10"
hardboard